Sew It Yourself
Home Decorating

Sew It Yourself Home Decorating

Creative Ideas for Beautiful Interiors

PRENTICE HALL PRESS • NEW YORK

Crochet abbreviations as used in this book

bk	back
ch	chain
dc	double crochet
ft	front
rep	repeat
sl st	slip stitch
sp(s)	space(s)
st(s)	stitch(es)

Photographic credits

Belinda: 8, 20, 31, 48, 51, 57, 58/59, 68, 82, 85, 87, 124, 128
Steve Bicknell: 61, 64
Simon Butcher: 154
Clive Corless: 17, 18
Rod Delroy: 94, 96
Ray Duns: 12
Robert Enever: 44/45
Jean-Paul Frogett: 73
Geoffrey Frosh: 135
Clive Helm: 117
Ron Kelly: 97
Tom Leighton: 33
Nigel Messet: 8, 149, 164
Michael Murray: 10
Ian O'Leary: 7
Spike Powell: 52, 81, 100/101, 120/121, 122, 130, 150, 153, 160
Peter Pugh-Cook: 75
Malcolm Robertson: 34, 78/79
Kim Sayer: 54/55, 70, 71, 106/107
Steve Tanner: 156
Jerry Tubby: 133
Gary Warren: 24/25, 27, 112, 115, 123, 141
Simon Wheeler: 113
Elizabeth Whiting: 2, 4, 8, 13, 21, 36, 38/39, 40, 41, 43
Paul Williams: 90/91
Graham Young: 145, 146

First Prentice Hall Press Edition, 1986

Published by Simon & Schuster, Inc.
Gulf + Western Building
One Gulf + Western Plaza
New York, NY 10023

Originally published by Arco Publishing, Inc.

PRENTICE HALL PRESS is a trademark of Simon & Schuster, Inc.

Manufactured in Singapore by Times Printers Sdn. Bhd.

Library of Congress Cataloging-in-Publication Data
Main entry under title:

Sew it yourself home decorating.

1. Sewing. 2. House furnishings. 3. interior decoration—Amateurs' manuals. I. Publishing.
TT715.S46   1984   646.2'1   84-9358
ISBN   0-13-807264-7

CONTENTS

CHAPTER 1

CHAPTER 2

CHAPTER 3

CHAPTER 4

CHAPTER 5

INTRODUCTION

Redecorating your own home may require a great deal of time and effort, but it is also one of the most exciting and rewarding tasks you can undertake; any money you save as a consequence is simply an added bonus. Perhaps the most important consideration is that you have total control over the extent and method of decorating. And you are under no pressure in terms of time other than deadlines you yourself set. When dealing with the problem as one of home furnishings you have an enormous amount of flexibility: you can upgrade an existing style by simple additions to a room; change the look or feel of a room by redoing everything from the draperies and slipcovers to the rugs; or, if you are really ambitious, you might consider tackling the whole house or apartment, item by item, room by room. The possibilities are endless – the approach you take is up to you.

Having made the decision to transform all or part of your home, you need a basic stock of ideas you can use or adapt and the simple know-how to implement those ideas. *Sew It Yourself Home Decorating* contains a wealth of material that deals with virtually every aspect of home furnishings. No room or area of the home is neglected and each project is illustrated in full color, with photographs to inspire and detailed diagrams to guide you carefully through every single step. Any special techniques which may be required are highlighted and explained concisely and clearly.

The projects range from adding a designer touch to an existing item – by monogramming towels or pillowcases, for example – to making bold rugs and slipcovers for your upholstered furniture. Make a careful list of everything you would like to change and a realistic plan of the most practical way to achieve your aim, taking costs and time into account. Then, with a little help from *Sew It Yourself Home Decorating*, you could soon be turning your home into your castle!

Chapter 1

Drapes, curtains and shades

Curtain know-how

Lined curtains

Cross-over curtains

Sheer elegance

Café curtains

Roman shades

Austrian curtains

Shower curtains

Curtain Know-How

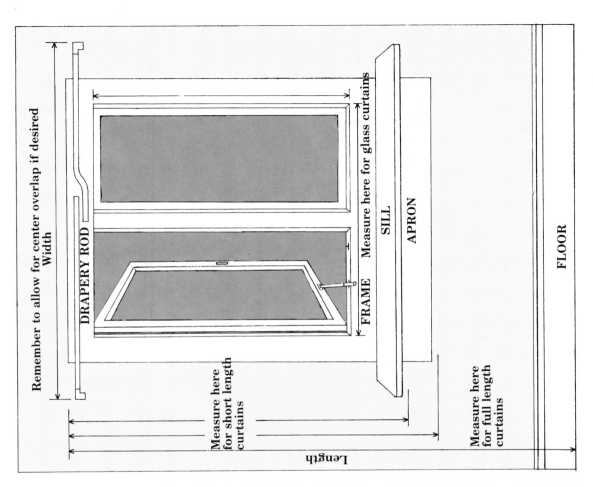

Remember to allow for center overlap if desired
Width

DRAPERY ROD

Measure here for glass curtains

SILL

APRON

FRAME

Measure here for short length curtains

Length

Measure here for full length curtains

FLOOR

Making your own drapes and curtains is one of the biggest money-savers in home sewing. All the drapery hardware on the market today makes it a fairly simple job, giving you the freedom of choice in style and fabric to achieve a professional, individual look to suit each room in your home.

Choosing the style

Before buying any fabric or sewing your first stitch, consider the style, length and color of drapes that will best suit your windows and complement the room. This is partly a question of personal taste and the style of your furnishings. If you have a modern home with contemporary furniture, ornate brocades and rich damasks would look completely out of place. If you prefer a Victorian or Colonial look, then consider a fabric that reflects the right period flavor. Besides the style of your home, there are a number of basic design points you should consider:

Size of room Generally, large designs and bold colors look best in a large room. But remember that too much pattern can be visually boring, so it is important to achieve the correct balance between the size of the room and the size of the design. Similarly, small designs and soft colors are best for small rooms, such as bedrooms.

Kind of room Consider what the room is used for and whether you spend a lot of time in it. For rooms with a functional use, such as bathrooms and kitchens, curtains should be in a practical fabric that is steam-resistant, that will wash and wear well, and be made in a casual style. In contrast, for rooms that are used less, such as the living room, dining room or bedroom, the curtains or drapes could be made in a more luxurious fabric and in a somewhat more elegant style.

Size and shape of windows Windows come in all shapes and sizes; some are tall and narrow, some short and wide. They may be arranged in uneven groups. Use drapes to their best advantage, covering the entire wall if necessary, so that when drawn they disguise rather than accentuate window irregularities.

There are basically three lengths to choose from – sill length, below the sill or floor length. Sill length curtains should just clear the sill and floor length drapes should finish 1in from the floor to protect from wear.

Measuring your windows

☐ Decide on the length of drapes you require and measure following the diagram as a guide. Add 8in for hems and headings.

☐ Measure the width of your windows, adding a further 1½in for each side hem. Decide on which style you require and multiply by the following to allow for fullness.

Standard gathered – allow one and a half times the width of the drapery rod.

Pinch pleats or cartridge pleats – allow twice the width of the drapery rod for fullness.

Pencil pleats – allow two and a half times the width of the drapery rod.

☐ Divide the width measurement by the width of the fabric you are buying to give you the number of fabric widths required in your curtains, allowing an additional 1in for each join required. Always round measurements up to the nearest width.

☐ Multiply the length measurement by this total. This will give you the total amount of fabric required.

Note If your fabric is not pre-shrunk, add approximately 1in per yard for shrinkage to the overall requirements.

Pattern-matching

If the fabric which you have chosen has a pattern that repeats itself, the patterns will have to be matched so that they run at the same level on all the curtains or drapes. This means buying extra fabric. Measure the pattern repeat and allow for one pattern repeat per width after the first; i.e., if three widths of material are required for the window, purchase extra material for two pattern repeats.

Fabrics and hardware

When buying fabrics always head for the upholstery fabrics department. As attractive as the designs or prices of dress fabrics may be, the fabrics themselves are just not durable enough, lacking body and qualities such as resistance to sunlight required of upholstery fabrics.

The following fabrics are suitable for drapes and curtains: velvet, brocade, chintz, cotton sateen, damask, percale, rep, taffeta, gingham and homespun. Always check if the fabrics are preshrunk, as this will affect the amount you buy.

Fabrics which are suitable for drapes include – cotton sateen, cotton rep, damask, chintz, homespun, brocade, gingham and velvet.

Lining

All types of drape are best lined to improve the hang, give added insulation and lengthen the life of the drapes by protecting the fabric from dirt and sunlight. Cotton sateen is the most commonly used lining fabric. Check that it is pre-shrunk to prevent any uneven shrinkage during laundering. The same rules apply to the purchase of lining as apply to the main drapery fabric. Do not try to economize by buying cheap fabric that may spoil the finished effect. Choose a suitable lining to match the curtain fabric. White, light beige or soft gray are neutral colors and the ones chosen most often.

Types of rod

There are two main categories of drapery rod. One is a standard rod designed to be hidden by the top of the drapes. The other is decorative and designed to be used so that the drapes hang just beneath it. The best headings to use with a decorative rod are pencil, cartridge and pinch pleated.

Drapery hardware

It is the finishing touches, like the use of weights or the fitting of a set of cords to draw the drapes, that will help to achieve a "professional" finish.

Weights can be purchased individually or on a string. Lead-weight tape is the best and the most up-to-date product to use and is available in three weights for different fabrics. Simply insert it along the bottom hem of your drapes and baste the hem at each end in order to secure it.

Drapes can become shabby and distorted over a period of time due to a great deal of handling. To prevent this it is sensible to use cords, which will add the final touch of luxury to your windows in addition to making the job of opening and closing them easier.

Headings

Drapery-making has been greatly simplified by the special tapes that can now be purchased to produce different headings that will cover the drapery track and take the place of a pelmet or valance. The pictures here show the

Types of headings

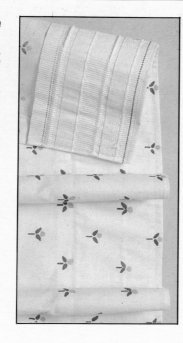

Cartridge pleated. The deep heading tape produces single pleats at 4in intervals, which form attractive regular folds. For use with decorative drapery rods, there is a special underslung version.

Pencil pleated. A deep stiffened tape is used for this type of heading. It creates identical, closely-spaced pleats that have a very classic, tailored look.

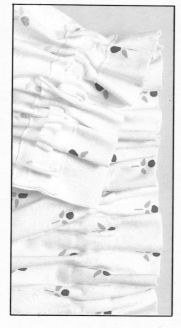

Standard gathered tape. When this tape is applied and the cords of the tape are pulled up, soft gathers are formed. This is a very versatile heading, suitable for all types of drapery fabric.

Pinch or triple pleated. Special long-pronged hooks are inserted into a deep pleater tape, to produce fanned pleating in regular groups.

Lined Curtains

First measure your windows and assess your fabric requirements following the method described on page 11, and buy the appropriate drapery fabric, lining fabric, heading tape and matching sewing thread.

Cutting out

Press fabric to remove all creases and carefully examine it for any flaws. Lay out the fabric on a large flat surface, then straighten the edges. To do this, mark a line at a right angle to the selvage (if possible, draw a thread as a guideline). On full-length drapes try to get an unbroken pattern repeat at the top, since the hem will be less noticeable. On short-length curtains the reverse applies and the pattern repeat should be unbroken at the hem.

□ Cut the first length; then if using a patterned fabric, cut all additional lengths using this first length as a guideline to ensure patterns match at the seams (fig. 1). Press and cut out the lining to the same measurements as the curtain or drapery pieces.

Joining lengths of fabric

□ Making sure that all fabric patterns run in the same direction, pin them together, taking 1–1¼in seams. Machine-stitch, using a fairly long stitch (fig. 2).

□ If you are making two curtains or drapes and an uneven number of fabric widths are used, one width will have to be cut in half lengthwise. Join this fabric width in half lengthwise, using the selvage to make the seam, the raw edge the side hem.

The wider fabric widths should be placed to the center of the window, the half widths at the side. Overcast raw edges. Press (fig. 3).

□ To release any tension in the fabric, the selvage should be snipped at approximately 4in intervals throughout (fig. 4). Join drape lining pieces in the same way. Press.

Hemming

□ Turn under 1½in hem at the sides of the drape, baste and press. Catch-stitch invisibly to curtain (fig. 5). Snip into any selvages.

□ For the foot hem, turn under ½in and press. Turn under a further 4in, pin and press (fig. 6).

□ Where the foot hem and side hems meet, there will be a superfluous thick-

ness of material, which must be removed by mitering to make a flat hem. Miter the hem at each corner as follows: At point A on bottom hem mark intersection with side hem (fig. 7a). Open out foot hem and cut into side hem to point B along foldline (fig. 7b). Fold hem from point B to A (fig. 7c). Fold foot hem back into position and note superfluous triangle at B. Snip this away (fig. 7d). Trim side hem allowance to 1½in (fig. 7e). Turn under the first turning of the hem and another small triangle is also formed. Snip this away (fig. 7f).

□ Fold hem back into position and then slipstitch hem to drape, being careful that no stitches show on the right side. Slipstitch mitered corners to side hems (fig. 8).

□ Turn under foot hem of the lining by ½in. Press. Turn under a further 5in. Slipstitch in place. Turn under corners or make side hems in the lining at this stage (fig. 9).

Locking in the lining

□ A lining is locked to thick drapery fabrics to prevent the lining from falling away from the top fabric when the curtain is hanging. Locking is usually worked at 12in intervals across a drape and should begin and end 8in from both bottom and top.

□ Place the drape on a flat surface with wrong side facing up. Lay the lining on top of the drape, wrong sides together, placing the hem edge of the lining 1-2in above the drape hem edge (fig. 10). On each single-width drape,

48in wide, make three rows of locking, one down the middle of the drape and one to each side, 12in from the edge.

□ Sew loop stitch as follows: fold back the lining along the center; join the thread to hem. Spacing stitches about 2in apart, pick up one thread of lining fabric and one of drape, having thread under needle to form a loop stitch (fig. 11). Complete the other two rows, one each side of the center row.

□ When the locking is completed, lay the lining flat again, turn in the side edges and pin to the drape so that ¾in of drape is showing. Slipstitch lining to drape at the two sides. Make a line of basting stitches 6in from the top to hold the lining firmly in place until the heading tape is attached (fig. 12). Trim any excess lining above the drape.

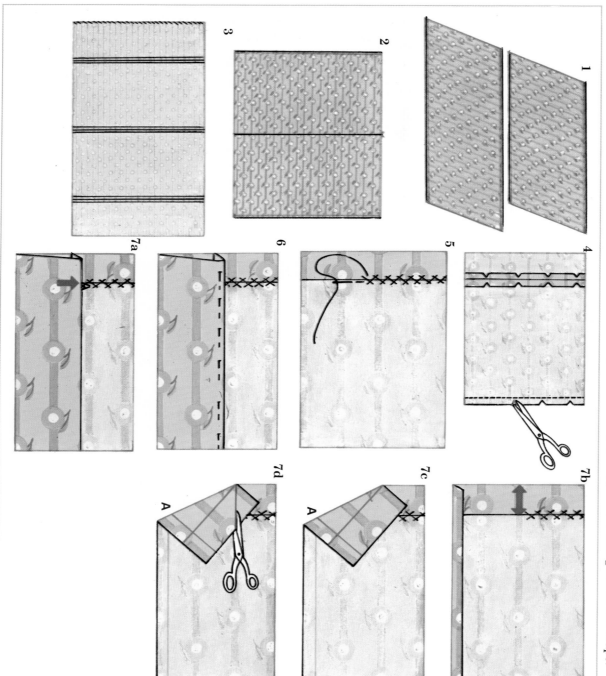

Attaching heading tape
Standard heading tape

☐ Turn over a ⅝in hem at the top of the drape, treating lining and drape as one. Baste (fig. 13). Cut the heading tape to drape width plus 1in each end.

☐ Pull out 1½in of cord from end of tape and tie it into a firm reef knot. This edge should be positioned on the side of the drape that comes to the center of the track. At other end, pull cords out 1½in and leave them free for pleating. Baste tape to drapes leaving ⅛in between top of tape and top of drape. Turn under both ends of tape to finish, making sure unknotted ends are left free (fig. 14).

☐ Machine-stitch tape to drape on both long edges, stitching in the same direction to avoid puckering. Stitch across short ends, securing cord ends by sewing in a few reverse stitches. On some drapery tapes a stitching guideline is woven into the tape (fig. 15).

☐ Finally press the drapes. Gather or pleat each drape by pulling the drawstrings from the side of each drape to the required width. Spread the gathers evenly and then tie them securely in a double bow or wind them onto a purchased cord holder (fig. 16). Do not cut off any surplus cord, so that drapes can be pulled flat when they are washed or dry cleaned. Insert curtain hooks at 3in intervals with a hook at each end.

Deep heading tapes

☐ Make drapes in the same way as when applying standard heading tape, and place top edge of tape ⅛in from the top of the drape.

Triple or cartridge pleater

☐ Allow enough extra tape on each drape so that half a space between pleats will be situated at each edge when drapes meet in the center. This will make sure that spaces are equally distributed when the drapes are pulled closed. If you are thinking of hanging drapes from a rod which is fixed from the ceiling, you should use underslung pleater tape.

Pencil pleating

☐ Apply heading tape as for triple or cartridge-pleated headings. If using a decorative rod or ceiling-fixed rod, sew the tape onto the fabric with the pockets at the bottom of the tape. The hooks will then be low enough so that the heading is able to clear the face of the rod.

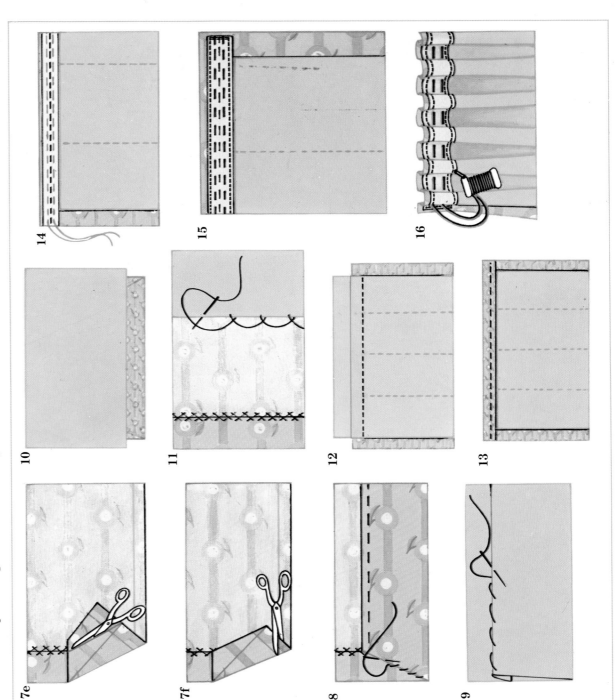

Cross-over Curtains

Sheer ruffled curtains give an appealing, fresh look to a window. You can make them either short or long, let them hang straight or tie them back or – for a lavish look – drape one over the other.

Ruffles can be used on most types of curtains but are most usual on curtains in sheer fabrics which tie back, sometimes crossing over in the center. The depth of the ruffle should be in proportion to the curtain and window size; for example, a very deep ruffle would not normally be used on a small window. As a general rule, ruffles are about 3–6in deep.

Making ruffled curtains

☐ Before you can estimate the fabric required you must calculate the cutting size of the ruffle. Decide on the finished ruffle depth required and add 1in for hems.

☐ To determine the length of the ruffle allow between two and a half and three times the finished ruffle length (usually the sum of one side and bottom edge of the curtain, as these are the edges ruffled on most curtains). If several pieces have to be joined to make the ruffle, add small seam allowances for each join.

☐ Measure the width and depth of the window and calculate the size of the curtain as you would for one without ruffles. Add 1½–2in to the width for the side hems and add small seam allowances if panels of fabric have to be joined. From this total, subtract the width of the curtain itself. To determine the cutting length of the curtain, take the finished length, then add ⅝in for a bottom hem and a suitable allowance for the type of heading you are using. From this total, subtract the depth of the finished ruffle.

☐ Cut out the curtains and the ruffle pieces to the measurements you have obtained. Always cut the ruffle as long as possible to avoid too many seams showing through to the right side. Join the panels for the curtains if necessary. If ruffle pieces have to be joined, be sure to use narrow interlocking fell seams.

☐ The ruffle can be attached to the curtain in either of two ways, depending on the heading used.

Ruffles on plain cased curtains

Turn under and stitch a narrow double hem on one long edge of the ruffle (fig. 1). On the other long edge, run two rows of gathering stitches close to the raw edge. Pull up the gathering threads until the ruffle fits the edges of the curtain (fig. 2).

☐ Pin and baste the ruffle to the curtain with right sides together and gathers evenly distributed. Stitch the two pieces together between the two lines of gathering stitches (fig. 3).

☐ Press the hem allowance toward the curtain. On the right side topstitch close to the seam through all thicknesses. Finish the seam if necessary (fig. 4).

Ruffles on headed cased curtains

☐ Turn under and stitch narrow double hems on both edges of the ruffle. Baste and stitch narrow double hems to the right side on the inner and bottom edges of the curtain (fig. 1).

☐ Run a row of gathering stitches 1in from one long edge on the ruffle. Pull up the gathering threads to fit the two edges of the curtain (fig. 2).

☐ Pin the ruffle to the curtain with right sides facing upward and the gathering stitches over the hem on the curtain. Make sure the ruffle is evenly distributed around both edges and does not look flat at the corner. Stitch ruffle in place, working over the gathering threads on the right side (fig. 3).

Finishing

Turn under and stitch double hems at the outer curtain edge. Turn under and stitch the casings at the top of the curtain as illustrated on page 19, extending the casing across the ruffle.

Cross-over tie-backs

Tie-back curtains or drapes which cross each other for part or all of the window width give a lavish look to the window at relatively low cost, and they are not difficult to make. Success ultimately depends on how well the fabric drapes. Sheer fabrics are ideal for cross-overs because the folds of the curtain underneath can be seen through those of the curtain on top. Generally, cross-overs are finished with a ruffle, and the instructions that follow are for ruffled cross-overs. However, you may adapt them for plain cross-overs by not subtracting the ruffle allowances and by adding, instead, allowances for two side hems and a lower hem.

Cross-over curtains

☐ To estimate the total fabric width needed for the window, first decide where you want the curtains to cross. Then measure the finished, gathered length of one of the curtains. For example, if the curtain rod is 80in long and each curtain will go across two-thirds of the track, the finished, gathered width of each curtain is about 53in. Subtract the depth of the ruffle. Double the resulting figure (for the two curtains), then multiply it by 2 or 3 for the desired fullness. Add 4in for outer side hem allowances and 1in for each seam if fabric panels have to be joined.

☐ Estimate the length of the curtains by measuring from the rod to ½in above the floor, if you are making floor length curtains or drapes, or to the sill or just below it for short curtains. Add a top heading allowance, and subtract the depth of the ruffle.

☐ If your windows are very wide and you want the curtains to cross over the entire width, you may have to cut the inside edge longer than the outside edge in order to have enough fabric to drape. Pin one end of a piece of string to the window frame where the inner edge of the curtain will start. Drape the string over to the side of the window where the curtains will be held by the tie-back, allowing the fullness desired (fig. 1).

☐ Decide on the finished curtain length below the tie-back and mark this point on the string. Measure the string to find the finished curtain length. Add a heading allowance to this figure, and subtract the depth of the ruffle. Estimate the length of the outer edge without draping, in the normal way.

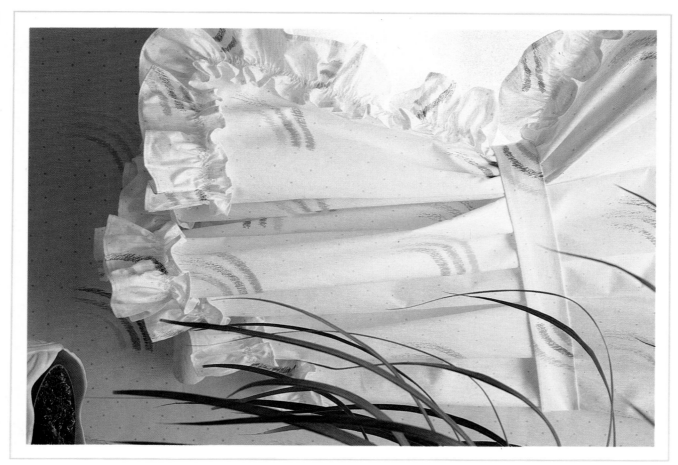

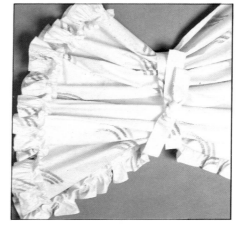

□ Cut out all the widths of fabric to the longer length and join the panels for each curtain. On one curtain mark the shorter measurement on the outside edge. Chalk a diagonal line to join this point to the inner corner of the curtain. Trim away the fabric below the line (fig. 2).

□ Cut out the other curtain using the first as a pattern, placing the right sides together and making sure that any pattern in the fabric is level on both curtains. (Note that this method is suitable only for curtains with ruffles, because a deep hem will not hang properly if turned up on a diagonal.)

□ Add ruffles as described. Hem the outer sides of each curtain. (Or hem both sides and the lower edge, if you are making plain curtains.)

□ Turn under and stitch the headings separately on each curtain if you wish to use a double rod.

□ Since it is easier to attach a single rod to the wall, you may prefer this method. If so, lay the two curtains together with right sides upward, overlapping them by the amount required. Double-check that they still fit the width of the window (fig. 3).

□ Turn under and stitch a casing along the whole width of the curtains, treating the double fabric where the curtains overlap as a single layer so that the two curtains will thread onto one rod.

Tie-backs

Tie-backs are the finishing touch to ruffled curtains and should be made with the size and style of the curtains in mind. We give instructions for simple tie-backs, but you can, if you prefer, make shaped or ruffled tie-backs.

□ To determine how long your tie-backs should be, hang the curtains up and loop a tape measure around the curtain, draping it to the side of the window. Allow sufficient room in the tie-back for the curtains to hang well. Add another ¾in for seam allowances to the finished length of the curtain tie-back (fig. 1).

□ Decide on the width of the tie-back. Make a paper pattern of the finished dimensions and try it against the curtains. Make any necessary adjustments. Add ¾in for seam allowances to the finished width measurement of the curtain.

□ Cut out two strips of fabric to the measurements you have estimated for each tie-back. Stitch the two pieces together along the long edges taking ⅜in seams and making sure that the right sides are facing (fig. 2). Trim seam allowances and turn strip right side out.

□ Turn in the seam allowances on the short ends and slipstitch the folded edges together. Attach a small ring near each end of the tie-back (fig. 3). Fix a small hook to the window frame to hold the tie-back in place. Make the other tie-back for the other side in the same way.

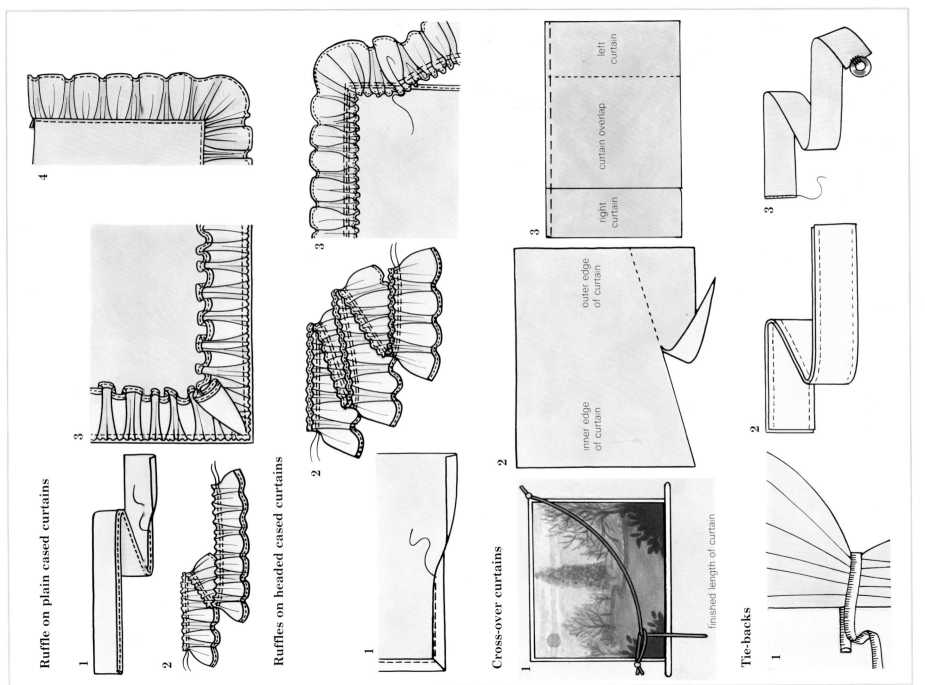

Ruffle on plain cased curtains

1 2 3 4

Ruffles on headed cased curtains

1 2 3

Cross-over curtains

1 finished length of curtain

2 inner edge of curtain outer edge of curtain

3 right curtain curtain overlap left curtain

Tie-backs

1 2 3

Sheer Elegance

Light and elegant, these lovely curtains demonstrate what sheer fabrics can do for a window. An amazing variety of effects can be created with sheers, used by themselves or along with drapes, shades or shutters.

Fabrics

Very fine glass curtains are available in several synthetic fibers which are resistant to shrinking and fading. These include polyester, nylon, and fiberglass. Semi-sheer fabrics, which are usually acrylic, generally have a more open weave and coarser texture than fine nets. Cotton lace, lawn and marquisette intended for use as curtains all look very attractive when made and hung.

Ready-made curtains are available in several standard drops, or lengths, and these are usually hemmed, and sometimes cased, by the manufacturer so that allowances are only needed for the side hems

The fabric width is actually the curtain length. After selecting the width corresponding to the curtain length you need (remembering to allow for a casing if needed), you should buy enough fabric to go across the window two or three times. Then it is just a simple matter of finishing the side edges and hanging the curtains

Here we describe the fabrics and techniques you need to know about when making glass curtains. Simple instructions explain how to make them with tape heading and with casings.

Obviously, glass curtains can only be used by themselves if the window is in a secluded area or if full privacy is not required. If you need to be able to cover the window completely, a shade or ordinary drapes may be used as well.

Sheer fabrics with interesting designs, like the ones shown here, are normally used by themselves. The pattern and texture of the fabric itself is heightened by the play of sunlight through it. Modern rooms with picture windows lend themselves particularly well to this treatment, though it can also be used effectively in traditional rooms. If you choose a glass curtain in a warm-toned fabric, the adjacent walls and ceiling will be bathed in a lovely warm glow whenever the sun shines.

Glass curtains are usually used along with heavier, lined draw drapes in order to give some privacy when the main drapes are opened. Glass curtains are stationary and are usually hung from a rod by means of a casing in the top of the curtain. Plain sheer fabrics can also be trimmed with ruffles and tied back for a draped effect – a style most often used on a bedroom window.

Headings

Tape headings

Glass curtains can be headed in the same style as curtains made from heavier fabrics. Special synthetic heading tapes are available which do not show too obviously on the right side of the curtain. Sheer fabrics look very attractive when made with deep heading tape for pinch and pencil pleats. The tapes may have cords to draw up the pleats, or slots to insert hooks.

If you plan to use a decorative rod use an underslung tape. Pinch pleats are the most suitable heading to use with a rod, as a ring can be attached behind every group of pleats.

The kind of tape you use will dictate the amount of fabric required, so decide on the heading before purchasing the fabric. The amount of tape needed must be calculated from the track width and not the width of the window. If the curtains are very wide you may need extra track at the side of the window to accommodate the fabric when the curtains are drawn back.

The manufacturer's guide to the amount of fullness required for the different tapes must be followed carefully, as buying less fabric may result in the curtains not being wide enough when the tape is drawn up.

Casings

An alternative heading for glass curtains is a simple casing. A casing is normally used on fine glass curtains which are to be fixed close to the window. Casings can be plain or headed. Headed casings have an extra fold of fabric above the casing which is gathered slightly when the curtains are drawn up on the rod.

For curtains which should not hang loose, such as those used on French doors and casement windows opening inward, make a casing on the bottom edge as well this can fit over a rod at the lower part of the window.

Stitching sheer fabrics

Glass curtains should always have double hems to prevent any uneven turnings from showing through. Baste the hems carefully before stitching, as they are likely to slip if the fabric is synthetic. If the fabric is very slippery or has a particularly open weave, place strips of tissue paper above and below the two layers of fabric before stitching and tear the tissue away afterward. A roller presser foot is

ideal for sewing lace fabrics, as it will not snag the fabric.

Hems can be stitched by hand or machine, using a fine needle and a sewing thread appropriate to the fabric. When stitching by machine, use long stitches and loosen the tension slightly to prevent pulling. And remember to make sure that your needle is sharp – a blunt one will pull the loosely-woven fabric.

Joining fabric widths

Fine glass curtains will generally hang better if the widths are not joined. Each panel can be hung separately and the selvages left unhemmed, as long as they are neat.

On other sheer fabrics which need to be joined use either a small French seam or an interlocking fell seam, as shown in the instructions for tape heading, which follow immediately.

On heavier fabrics like cotton lace, you can use an ordinary flat seam. Press the seams open. If the selvages pull, either snip them at intervals on both seam allowances or, before sewing the widths together, cut the selvages off completely. This will prevent the edges from puckering.

Using tape heading

These curtains are made in the same way as unlined curtains of heavier fabric, using one of the lightweight tapes described on page 12.

□ Estimate the fabric required, using fig.1 as a guide. Multiply your track length (A) by the manufacturer's fullness allowance for the tape you have chosen – usually between two and two and a half times the track width. Divide this figure by the width of the fabric you plan to use, rounding up the answer to the nearest whole width, to give you the number of fabric widths you need to buy. Add 12in for both bottom hems and top to the finished length of curtain (B). Multiply the total length by the number of fabric widths needed to obtain the amount of fabric required. If you are using patterned fabric, allow extra for matching the design as described on page 11. Cut out the curtains.

□ Join the fabric widths with flat seams, French seams or interlocking fell seams. Remember, if the fabric is loosely woven and apt to sag, it is a good idea to clip the selvages first. For an interlocking fell seam, lay the two pieces to be joined with right sides together and with the edge of the bottom layer extending ¼in beyond the edge of the top layer down the length of the seam (fig. 2a). Turn the edge back over the top layer of fabric (fig. 2b). Fold both layers once more to form a seam ¼in wide. Stitch close to the inside fold. This gives an unobtrusive seam, with no stitching showing on the right side (fig. 2c).

□ Turn 1in to the wrong side along both sides of the curtain. Fold again to form a 1in-wide double hem. Baste and stitch in place by hand or machine.

□ Turn and press a single hem, the same depth as the curtain tape, to the wrong side at the top of the curtain. Baste the tape over the top of the curtain, making sure it is the correct way up and that the top edge of the tape is just below the fold. Leave a 1½in overlap of tape at each side of the curtain. If you are us-

ing pinch pleater tape, make sure that the set of pleats lying nearest the center of the window on each curtain is an equal distance from the edge on both curtains, if the curtains do not overlap in the middle of the window.

□ If you are using a tape with cords to draw up the pleats, pull out the cords at each end of the tape. Fold under the raw ends and stitch the tape in place at the center edges of the curtains. For curtains which are pleated with pronged hooks, finish the raw ends of the tape and stitch them in place. In either case, the two rows of stitching should be close to the edge of the tape (fig. 3).

□ Baste up double hems at the bottom of the curtain. They should be quite deep so that the curtains hang well. Do not stitch the hems, but hang the curtains from the rod for a day or two so

that the fabric drops. This is particularly important with loosely woven fabrics or if the fabric is heavy.

□ Make any necessary adjustments to the length of the curtains. Take them down. Trim the hem allowance to an even depth. Turn up half the hem allowance, then the other half. Pin and baste the hem in place and stitch it by hand or machine. Press.

□ To help the curtains hang perfectly use light weights. Insert the lightest weighted polyester tape available through the bottom hems and secure at the side edge only. Weights must be removed before cleaning or they will rust (fig. 4).

A plain casing

□ Measure the width and length of the window area the curtains will cover. Allow between two and three times the

Sheer curtains with a tape heading

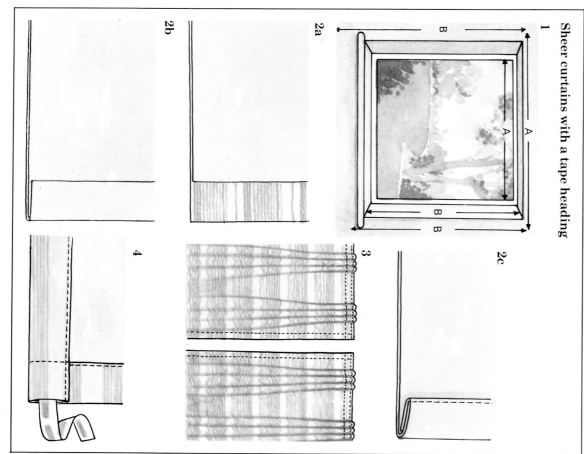

finished curtain width for fullness. To the finished curtain length, add between 7in and 8in for the bottom hem and 3in for the top casing. Cut out fabric to these measurements, allowing ⅝in extra on each edge if widths have to be joined.

□ Turn the fabric under and carefully stitch narrow double hems at the sides of the curtain.

□ Turn 1½in to the wrong side at the top edge of the curtain. Fold over the top again to make a 1½in-wide double hem. Press and machine-stitch close to the lower fold in order to form a casing. Slide the casing over the curtain rod to make sure it can be accommodated easily (fig. 1).

□ Turn up the curtains to the correct length and baste a double hem in place at the lower edge. Hang the curtain from the rod so that you can check the length. After you have made any necessary last minute adjustments, then carefully machine-stitch the curtain hem in place.

A headed casing

□ Curtains with a headed casing are made in a similar way to curtains with a plain casing.

□ Estimate the width of the fabric required in the same way as for plain headed curtains. Add between 7in and 8in for the bottom hem to the finished length of the curtain. Allow twice the depth of the heading required, plus 3in for the casing itself. The depth of the casing should be in scale with the size of the curtain. The longer the drop of the curtain, the deeper the heading may be.

□ Turn the fabric under and stitch double side hems.

□ Fold half the allowance (including the casing allowance) at the top of the curtain to the wrong side. Fold again to form a double hem and stitch in place close to the bottom fold. Sew another line of stitching about 1in above the first line.

□ Turn up the bottom hems, check the length and stitch in place. If the fabric is at all heavy, it is best to leave the curtains to hang for two or three days; this way the fabric can drop out to its real length before you finally adjust the hem.

Note If you are making curtains with casings at top and bottom – for example, for French doors – be sure to check the length carefully before you stitch the casings in place, so that the curtains cover the area smoothly, neither pulling nor drooping between the rods.

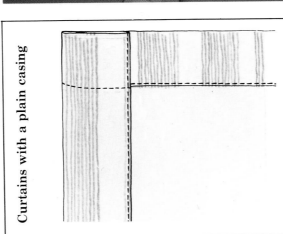

Curtains with a plain casing

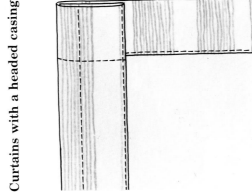

Curtains with a headed casing

Café Curtains

No wonder café curtains are so popular – their informality makes a room seem warm and welcoming and at minimal cost, too. Here we give you detailed instructions for making café curtains with a scalloped heading, plus tips on making other variations on the café curtain theme.

Café curtains are a good way of hiding an ugly view or obtaining more privacy while still letting in the light, as they usually cover only the bottom half of a window. You can vary the basic style of café curtains in an amazing number of ways. For example, you can make two-tier café curtains and open the upper tier during the day and close it at night. You can add a shallow tier at the upper edge of the window. You can use café curtains along with full-length curtains, with a shade, with shutters or with a combination of shades and ordinary curtains.

□ It is also possible to make the curtains with various kinds of headings: a simple casing, a pinch-pleated heading, a scalloped heading or scallops combined with pleats. Fabric loops, for example, make a very stylish heading.

□ Café curtains can be made in most fabrics, though because of their informal style, they are not normally made in heavy, rich fabrics. Heavier fabrics can be lined with thin cotton if you wish. Café curtains made in sheer fabrics can create an effect which is particularly charming.

Measuring

□ First decide on the position of the curtain rod. This can be inside or outside the window recess, and is usually positioned halfway down the frame, al-

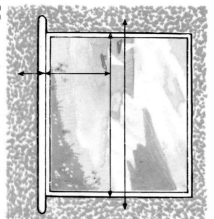

though this position can obviously be varied to suit different types of window (fig. 1). To make the window appear larger, fix the pole so that the finials (decorative ends) are outside the window frame.

□ Decide on the finished pole width, not including finials, that the curtains will cover.

□ Measure the curtain drop – the length from the rod to the finished hem. The hemline may be at sill level, just below the sill or even at floor level, if you have full length windows.

Estimating fabric

□ The type of heading you choose will dictate the width of fabric you need for the curtains and the resulting amount of fullness. If you are using drapery heading tape, follow the manufacturer's fabric allowance guide. Shaped headings will need between one and a half and two and a half times the rod length, depending on the fabric used. The more delicate the fabric, the more fullness will be required. The directions for making the curtains explain how to estimate fabric for a scalloped heading.

□ To the finished width add 2in for each side hem. Divide this total by the width of your chosen fabric to find the number of fabric widths you will need. If you are using heading tape, you may need to trim away some of the width. If not, you may be able to reduce or increase the fullness slightly in order to use whole widths of fabric.

□ Now calculate the length. Add 4in to the curtain drop for the bottom hem. The top heading may need between 4in and 8in, depending on whether you use a tape or a shaped heading. If you do use a shaped heading, draw up a pattern for the shape first (see 'Scalloped café curtains'), and measure the finished heading depth; then add 2in to this measurement to obtain the top heading allowance. The finished

length of the curtain, plus the heading allowance, is the cutting length of the curtains.

☐ Calculate how much fabric is required by multiplying the cutting length of the curtain by the number of widths of fabric. Allow extra fabric to match a large pattern – the upholstery salesperson can help you to calculate this.

Scalloped café curtains

Made in crisp cotton, these curtains have a scalloped and hand-pleated heading and are hung from the rod on rings. We give directions for making a pair of curtains, but you can easily make a single panel instead. This type of curtain would also look very pretty in a lacy or a gingham fabric.

☐ First plan the size of the scallops. These curtains have 4in-wide scallops placed 6in apart. The 6in margin measures only 2in when pleated. These measurements may be adjusted if necessary, but do not make the scallops too wide or they will lose their shape when the curtain is pleated. Calculate how many pleats and scallops you will fit across each curtain width and allow 4in of fabric per scallop, plus 6in for the pleated section, plus 2in hems at each side. You must have one more pleated section than you have scallops so that there are pleats at both ends.

☐ Now make a pattern for the scallops. On cardboard draw a circle with 4in diameter. Draw a line horizontally across the diameter and draw lines vertically upward from each end of this line to a depth of 6¾in. Join the two lines at the top, and cut out the pattern (fig. 2).

☐ Join the widths of fabric, matching the pattern if necessary, and finish the seams. Press them open (fig. 3).

☐ Press a ⅜in hem to the wrong side at the top edge to the curtain. Fold the top edge to the right side to a depth of 8in. Baste along the top and bottom edges of the hem (fig. 4).

☐ Starting at the left-hand edge of the curtain, allow 2in for a side hem, and then mark the top fold 6in from that point. This is the allowance for the first pleated section. Lay the pattern on the fabric, matching the top edge of the cardboard to the top fold and the side edge to the 6in mark. Draw around the pattern with tailor's chalk or soft pencil. Mark off the next 6in pleat allowance and draw the next scallop.

25

Continue in this way across the whole width of each curtain until the last pleat allowance marked (fig. 5).

□ Stitch down the side edges of the curtain heading almost to the bottom fold of the heading, 2in from the side edge. Stitch around each scallop on the marked line. Trim the scallop seam allowances and clip into the curves.

Trim away the side seam allowances ¼in from the stitching to eliminate unnecessary bulk (fig. 6).

□ Turn the scallops right side out and baste around each scallop close to the edge. Turn under a double 1in-wide hem down both sides of the curtain. The tops of both hems will be enclosed by the top heading (fig. 7). Catch-stitch the heading to the hem on each side.

□ Mark the finished curtain length by measuring from the top of the pleat allowances down the curtain. Turn up and stitch a 1in-wide double hem.

□ Fold the pleat allowance between each scallop into three equal pleats and stitch the three folds together on the right side, 4½in down from the top edge (fig. 8).

□ Attach a ring to the center pleat in each group (fig. 9). Thread the rings onto the curtain rod, positioning the end ring on each side between the finial and the bracket supporting the rod, to provide anchorage for the curtains.

Different headings

Fabric loops

Flat loops are made separately in matching fabric and attached to the top of the curtain (fig. 1).

Fabric loops and shaped headings are cut in one with the main curtain and are faced on the wrong side. The loops are stitched in place as shown (fig. 2). Narrow loops can be made from a bias-cut strip of fabric which can be continued along the top curtain edge as a binding (fig. 3).

Rings

Curtains pleated with curtain tape are usually attached to the rings with hooks. There is a wide range of tapes and hooks available in upholstery or notions departments. Alternately, the rings can be stitched to the center pleat in each group (fig. 4).

Split rings can be attached to the curtain through eyelets cut into the top of the curtain. To make the eyelets, you will need a special hole punch (fig. 5).

Café curtains

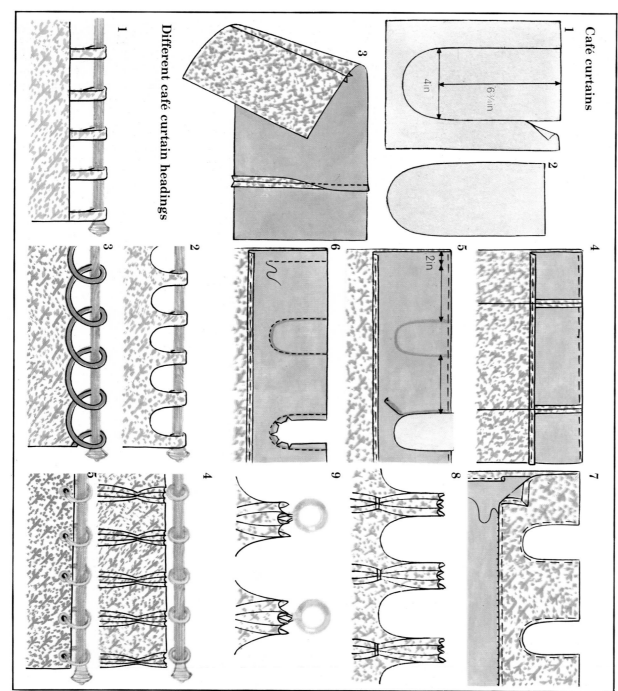

Different café curtain headings

Roman Shades

Roman shades combine the best features of drapes and window shades – soft folds and architectural simplicity.

Materials

Heavy cotton fabric and lining
2in by 1in battening
3/4in by 1/4in-wide wood for laths
Plastic curtain rings
Cord
Nylon tape
Matching sewing thread
1 cleat
2 L-shaped brackets
3 eyelet screws

Calculating the materials

☐ Measure the length and the width of window from the *outside* of the frame to the sill.

☐ For the amount of main fabric required: add 3in to the length for hems and seam allowances and 2in to the width for hems. For lining fabric: same amount, but with 3/4in for hems, plus 2¾in for each lath channel except bottom one. Allow 8in of main fabric to cover the batten.

☐ To work out how many laths will be needed, decide on the depth of the bottom section. All pleats will lie on top of this when the shade is up.

☐ The shade is divided horizontally into sections — the pleats are twice the depth of the bottom section. There is a lath at the bottom edge of the shade and one at the lower edge of each section. So if your bottom section is 6in deep, each pleat will be 12in deep. It looks smarter if the lath hangs beneath the pleats when the shade is up, so add 1½in to the bottom section measurement for this. At the top edge, make the pleat 3in deeper.

☐ To mount the shade, you will need a 2in by 1in batten, the width of the finished shade; the batten is attached to the wall with two L-shaped brackets. And you need a number of 1in by 1/4in laths, one for the lower edge and one for each pleat; each lath should be 1in shorter than the width of the finished shade.

☐ To pull shade: you need two plastic curtain rings per lath, except for bottom one, and a length of cord four times the length of the shade from second lath to top, plus width.

☐ A length of nylon tape, the width of the finished shade, attaches the shade to the batten. A cleat at one side of the window holds the cords when the shade is up.

Making the shade

☐ Cut lining to size. Turn under 3/8in

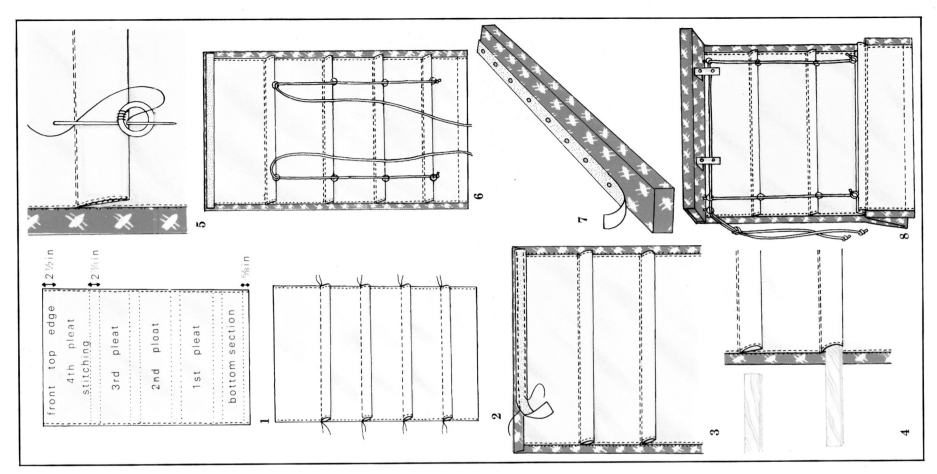

1

front top edge
4th pleat
stitching
3rd pleat
2nd pleat
1st pleat
bottom section

2½in
2½in
⅝in

2

3

4

5

6

7

8

along sides; pin, baste and stitch close to raw edge. On right side mark all stitching lines (fig.1).

□ To form channels for laths, bring pairs of stitching lines together with wrong sides facing, leaving bottom channel. Pin, baste and stitch along each line (fig. 2).

□ Center the lining over main fabric, right sides together. Pin, baste and stitch along bottom stitching line ⅝in from edge. Trim seam to ⅜in, turn right side out and press.

□ Turn under 1in along sides of main fabric. Lay lining and main fabric flat, wrong sides together and lining uppermost. Pin, baste and stitch lining to main fabric 1⅜in from bottom edge, forming first channel.

□ Pin, baste and stitch lining to main fabric just above stitching line of next channel. Repeat above each channel. Slipstitch lining to main fabric along sides, leaving channels open.

□ Turn under raw top edges ⅜in and baste. Cut length of nylon tape to width of finished shade. Place one side of it along top, ¹⁄₁₆in from folded edge, covering raw edges. Pin, baste and stitch close to edge. (fig.3).

□ Slip laths into channels and slipstitch to close ends (fig.4).

□ Sew two rings to each lath, except for bottom one, 4in from ends (fig.5).

□ Cut length of cord, twice the length of shade from second lath to top, plus width; cut second length twice the length of shade from second lath to top. Tie one cord to each bottom ring and thread through rings above (fig.6).

□ Cover batten with matching fabric. With small tacks, attach remaining side of nylon tape to top of batten at back edge. Fix two L-shaped brackets above window to hold batten in position. Fix two eyelet screws to underside of batten, 4in from each side to line up with rings on laths. Screw third eyelet screw into underside of batten ⅝in from one side edge (side on which shade is pulled). Fix batten to brackets (fig.7).

□ Fix cleat to side of window. Thread cords through corresponding eyelet screws and out to one side. Match up nylon tape and attach shade to batten. With shade hanging flat, knot cords together just past third eyelet screw. Pull up shade to form pleats and wind cords around cleat in a figure eight (fig.8).

Austrian Curtains

Austrian curtains, popularly called balloon shades, are the newest, prettiest way to dress windows. Their ruffles and soft scalloped effect add an instant designer touch to any decorating scheme.

Finished size

36in wide (without ruffle) and 90in long

Materials

6¾yd of 48in-wide fabric
15yd of bias binding
Matching sewing thread
2¾yd of drapery heading tape
Curtain hooks
5½yd of white cotton tape
26 white plastic curtain rings
24yd of white nylon cord
1 36in-long 2 × 1in wooden batten
4 picture ring screws
1 cleat

Choosing the materials

☐ When you pick a drapery heading tape, make sure that it suits the fabric and the room setting: for example, a pencil pleat tape looks good in a fairly elegant room, but a simpler tape would look better used on sheer fabrics. You can add ruffles or a lace edging to the sides and base of your shade or bind the edges in a contrasting color.

☐ Austrian curtains look particularly attractive in bedrooms and living rooms. Floral cotton prints and seersucker will produce a gentle, decorative effect, whereas bold graphic patterns will not harmonize well with the shade's soft scalloped lines.

☐ Luxurious fabrics such as moiré, taffeta, satin and chintz, in plain, rich colors, will look elegant and dramatic in large windows.

☐ Austrian curtains are also a good alternative to sheers to give an opulent look, for instance, in bathrooms. Make the curtains in voile using a light-weight tape.

☐ For the drapery heading, choose pencil pleat or standard curtain heading tape. The length should be the same as the full width of the ungathered blind plus 1in for finishing.

☐ Ordinary white cotton tape is appropriate for the vertical gathers. You will need the length of the blind by the number of tapes you want. Make sure

that the tapes are straight and equally spaced across the back of the shade. To avoid visible seams on the right side of the shade, iron them onto the shade using double-sided bonding tape.

☐ Cord is used for pulling up the gathers and is threaded through the rings at the back of the blind. White nylon cord is strong, but fairly thin, and will not show through. Estimate the amount you should buy by allowing 2½ times the length of each vertical tape.

☐ The track should be fixed to a batten (which you can buy from a lumber yard) so fix one above your window before you hang your blind.

☐ When measuring your window, always use a wooden yardstick or steel rule – this will ensure accurate measurements. Decide whether you want the shade to hang inside or outside the frame. For a shade hanging inside the frame, measure the inside length and width (A and B as shown). When measuring for a blind hanging outside the frame (C and D), extend the blind width by at least 2in on each side (fig. 1). You will need two or 2½ times the width in fabric to achieve the right fullness: the length is the same as the length of the window, plus approximately 8in. Also allow enough fabric for the ruffles.

Making the curtain

☐ Cut the fabric into as many lengths as necessary in order to gain the correct width, making sure that the fabric grain is straight and when stitched together the design will match. Pin, baste and stitch the lengths together with French seams (see panel). Turn under a ⅝in wide double hem along the side edges. Press and baste in place.

☐ Make a 3in wide strip of fabric twice the length of the blind: pin, baste and stitch strips together with narrow French seams to the required length. Cut bias binding to the same length as the fabric.

☐ Cut a length of bias binding the same length as the shade. Press flat, then press evenly in half lengthwise. Place one basted edge of the shade over the bias binding so that the folded edge of the binding extends ¼in outside the side edge of the shade.

☐ With right sides uppermost, position side edge of shade (with binding) over raw, gathered edge of ruffle. Pin, baste and topstitch down the side edge. Repeat on the other side (fig. 3).

☐ Mark the position of vertical tapes on the wrong side of the shade with rows on pins. Place the first two lengths at each side edge over raw edges, and the remaining tapes at equal intervals in between, about 10 to 12in apart. Pin, baste and stitch tapes to blind, close to each tape edge in marked positions.

☐ Turn under ⅜in along the top edge of the shade and press. Position a length of shade heading tape across the top edge of the blind, covering the raw edge of the fabric and tapes and turning under the raw ends. Knot the cord ends together at one side, leaving the cords free at the opposite end. Pin, baste and stitch the tape in place (fig. 5).

☐ Turn under a ⅝in hem along the bottom edge of the shade and press. Make a 5½in wide strip of fabric in the same way as side ruffles, twice the width of the shade, plus the width of both side ruffles. Cut the bias binding to the same length.

☐ Apply bias binding over the raw edge of the ruffle as for side ruffles. Run two rows of gathering stitches close together, ⅝in from the top edge of the ruffle. Gather the ruffle evenly to fit width of shade, including side ruffles, continuing your line of topstitching to join the edges of the side ruffle and base ruffle. Finish the side edges (fig. 6).

☐ Stitch curtain rings, about 8in apart, to the center of each tape (if not using tape with rings already attached). On the center tapes stitch the first row about 2½in above ruffle edge. On the side tapes, stitch the first row in line with the second row of the center tapes. Stitch the last row on all the tapes about 6in from the top. Make sure that all rings align horizontally (fig. 7).

☐ Fold bias binding evenly in half over bottom edge of ruffle strip, enclosing raw edges. Baste and stitch (fig. 2).

☐ Run two rows of gathering stitches close together, ⅝in from the top edge of the ruffle and pull up evenly to fit the side edge of the shade.

☐ Cut a length of bias binding the same length as the shade. Press flat, then press evenly in half lengthwise. Place one basted edge of the shade over the

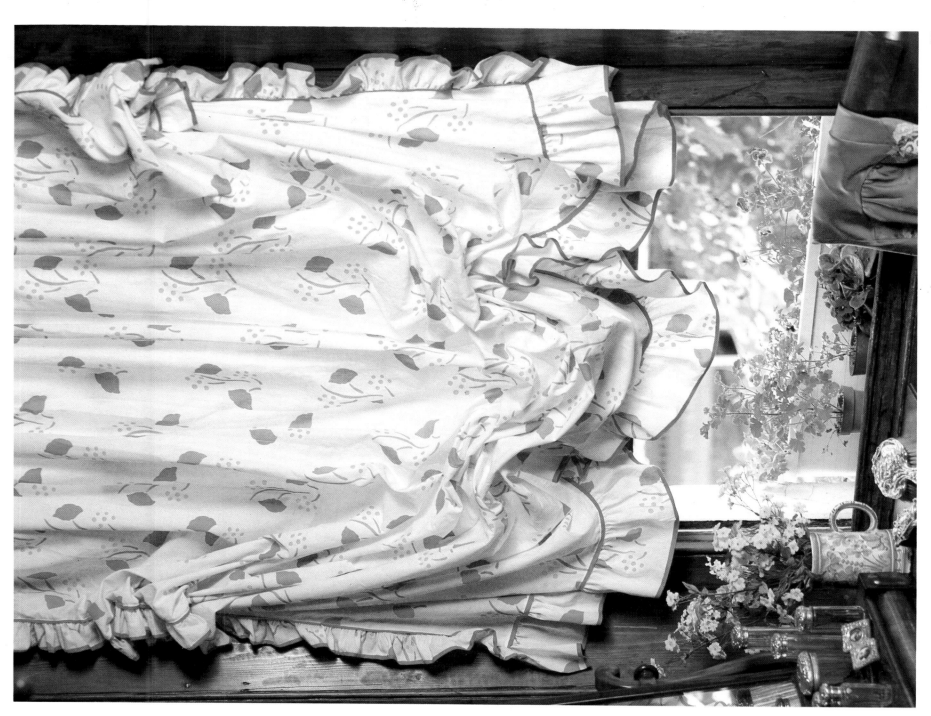

1

□ You may either paint the batten so that it matches the color of the window frame or cover it with fabric to match the curtains. Fix drapery track to front of batten.

□ Pull up gathering cord evenly in the drapery heading to fit track and knot together, but do not cut off. Slot curtain hooks into the heading.

Fix a picture ring screw into the base of the batten to correspond with each vertical tape.

Now cut lengths of nylon cord: cut the same number of cords as you have vertical tapes; each piece of cord should be equal to 2½ times the length of each vertical tape.

French seam

Place the two pieces of fabric to be joined with the wrong sides together. Pin and baste ⅝in from the edge. (This line will be the final stitching line). Stitch ¼in outside the basted line.

Remove the basting stitches. Press the seam open. Trim down the seam allowances to just under ¼in. Turn the work to the wrong side and fold over on the seam-line. Baste and machine stitch again, just outside the enclosed seam allowances.

2

3

4

5

6

7

8

☐ Mount the shade on the track, making sure to slot the curtain hooks at each end of the heading through the end stops on the track. This ensures that the shade will remain fixed in place. Now thread the left-hand cord through the row of screw eyes in the batten. Repeat with each length of cord. Let the cords hang free at the right-hand side (fig. 9).

☐ Fix the cleat onto the wall at the side of the window. Cut off the lengths of the cord even with the base of the shade. Knot the cord lengths together. Wind the cord round the cleat in a figure eight to hold. The shade is raised and lowered with these cords (fig. 10).

9

10

Shower Curtains

This pretty and practical shower curtain is made from a print fabric and lined with plastic to keep all the splashes in the tub!

Finished size
Approx. 93in wide × 70in long
Materials
4⅛yd of 48in-wide patterned drapery fabric
4⅛yd of 48in-wide plain white plastic
Matching sewing thread
2⅜in of 1in-wide standard drapery heading tape
Shower curtain hooks
Paper clips

□Trim the selvage edges off both sides of the patterned fabric: on one side, measure the width of the selvage and mark with a pin. Continue marking with pins down the marked line. Repeat on the opposite side of the fabric (fig. 1).

□Cut the fabric in half widthwise: then fold fabric in half and mark across the width with pins. Cut along the marked line.

□Place the fabric pieces with right sides together to match the center edges, making sure that the pattern runs in the same direction. Match the pattern design together and pin horizontally across the seamline to hold it firmly in position (fig. 2). Trim off any excess fabric at both top and bottom after matching the pattern.

□Baste and stitch the center seam, checking the pattern match as you stitch. Trim the seam down to ⅝in and press the seam open.

□On each side edge make a double hem by turning the raw edge to the wrong side for 1in. Turn the edge under again for 1in. Pin and baste in place. Repeat on the hem edge, mitering the bottom corners at the side edges. Stitch both sides and hem edge in position (fig. 3).

□Cut the plastic lining pieces in half widthwise; fold the fabric in half widthwise, matching edges. Keeping your hand firmly on the fold so the plastic does not slip, carefully cut through the fold.

□Place plastic lining pieces with non-shiny sides together, matching center edges. Hold together firmly with paper clips, spaced at about 6in intervals. Stitch the center seam, taking a ⅜in seam allowance and using a larger-than-average stitch. Refold, with shiny sides together and stitch center seam again, taking a ⅝in seam allowance, to form a French seam (fig. 4)

□On the wrong side of the plastic lining, measure the curtain width: measure width of the fabric curtain from the center seam to the side hem. Measure this figure plus 2in seam allowance on each side of the center seam on plastic lining and mark lightly with a soft pencil. Trim off excess fabric on each side down the marked lines.

□Hem the lining as for the curtain, but hold the hems in position with paper clips for stitching instead of pinning and basting.

□Position plastic lining on the fabric curtain with right sides together, matching top edges. Pin, baste and stitch together along top edge, taking 1⅛in seam allowance (fig. 5). Trim and turn curtains right side out.

□Position the top edges so that the lining comes just below the top fold and does not show on the fabric side of the curtain. Pin and baste along the top edge.

□Position the heading tape on the plastic lining side of the curtain. Butt one edge of the heading tape to the top folded edge of the curtain. Turn under the raw edges for ⅜in at each end of the tape, leaving the cord free. Pin, baste and stitch the heading tape in place (fig. 6).

□Pull up heading tape slightly. Slot the curtain hooks through the heading tape. Position a hook 1½in from the outer edge on each side. Fit the remaining hooks between the first two hooks, at 6in intervals. Slot the hooks over the shower rail.

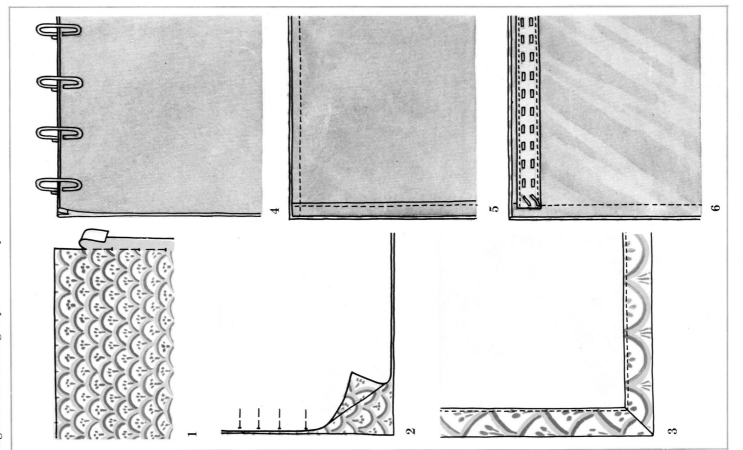

Chapter 2

Slipcovers and throw pillows

Slipcovers
Simple sofa
Chair bed
Kitchen chair seats
Sag bag
Bolsters
Appliqué pillows
Lace pillows

Slipcovers

Having a chair covered professionally can be very expensive. With these easy-to-follow directions, you too can become an expert – and give your furniture a real facelift!

Slipcovers are the best way to brighten up a worn armchair or sofa and, if well made, they can make an old piece of furniture look brand new. They also have the practical advantage of being removable for cleaning, so they maintain a crisp and clean appearance.

Slipcovers are not difficult to make, provided you have basic sewing skills, so do not be put off by the overwhelming size of the task. However, you will need plenty of time, patience and a large area in which to work.

Preparing the chair

With the exception of leather and vinyl upholstery, almost any armchair or sofa can be given a new lease of life with slipcovers. However, they will not hide lumps, bumps or broken chair springs, so before starting the job, take a good look at the chair you want to cover. If the cushions have lost their shape and the filling has gone limp, consider replacing them. If the furniture is secondhand, scrutinize it for woodworm and treat accordingly. Even if the chair is sound, give it a spring cleaning by vacuuming thoroughly. If necessary, shampoo the upholstery.

Choosing a suitable fabric

Tough, firm, closely woven fabrics such as cotton (chintz, for example) or linen are best for slip covers. Pick a fabric that is washable or can be dry cleaned, is colorfast and preshrunk. If uncertain about shrinkage, wash or clean the entire fabric before cutting out.

Very thick fabrics are best avoided, as they are difficult to work with and their bulk at seams makes it almost impossible to achieve a smooth-fitting cover. Fabric design must also be care-fully considered. If the design repeat is more than 24in fabric will be wasted matching the design and centering it on cushions, so it is an uneconomical buy. Repeats of 12in are more practical but can still be overwhelming if they are used on a small chair.

Remember, bold fabrics will dominate a room, whereas small prints will blend with existing furnishings. Solid color fabrics are the easiest and most economical to work with, as there is no matching to do. Check also for nap: velvet, for instance, should always be made into covers with the nap smoothed down.

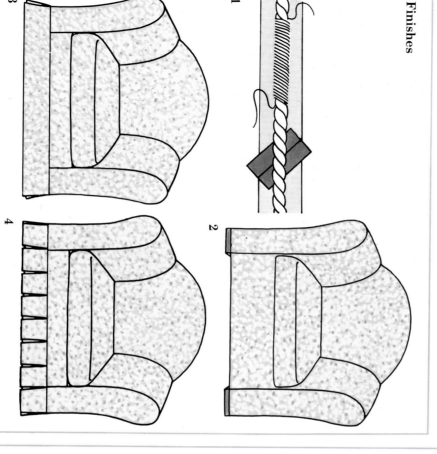

3

4

1

2

Finishes

Finishes

Piping – this improves the appearance of a slip cover, but if you have no experience with this sewing method, or if your sewing machine is unable to cope with four thicknesses of fabric, it would be better to make the cover without piping. The best way to calculate the quantities of piping cord is simply to measure the existing seams on the old cover. As a guide, a sofa takes about 44yd of cord, so allow at least an extra 2yd of fabric for covering the cord. For a slipcover for a chair, you must allow at least 22yd of cord and an extra 1yd of the covering fabric.

To pre-shrink new piping cord before use, wind the cord into a hank, then boil it or put it through a hot machine cycle and dry as quickly as possible.

To join two pieces of piping cord, unravel the strands slightly at each end and trim each strand to a different length. Wind the strands together, then bind the join with threads.

To cover the piping cord, cut out 1⅛in-wide bias strips of fabric. Join the fabric strips together with seams on the straight of grain (fig. 1). Fold the fabric in half, wrong sides together around the cord; pin and baste firmly in place.

Skirts – covers can be finished with a fitted base and simply tied under the chair (fig. 2). For a fitted base, add 6in to the length of sides, front and back for a turn-under allowance and for the hem.

☐ A plain skirt can be added to the cover, with box pleats at each corner (fig. 3). Skirts are usually 6in deep, but measure the size against the chair. To calculate the fabric needed for a plain skirt, decide on the depth and add 4in for seam allowances and hem. Measure around the chair back, front and sides and add 14in to each measurement for corner pleats.

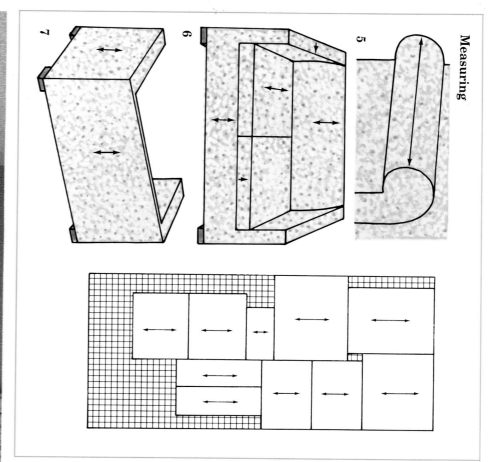

5

6

7

□ Another finish is a skirt with box pleats or a gathered ruffle (fig. 4). The depth of the skirt will be the same as the plain skirt. Measure all around the chair and multiply the figure by three, adding ¾in for seam allowances.

Measuring the chair.

When measuring and making the cover, work to the existing seamlines on the original upholstery.

□ On scroll armchairs there will be an additional seam along the outside arm to improve the fit of the cover (fig. 5).

□ Always take the measurements at the widest part of the chair.

□ Add 1½in to each measurement for a ¾in seam allowance.

□ The 4in tuck-in allowance (see diagram) is for the extra fabric that is tucked in between the chair back, arms and seat to hold the slipcover in place.

□ For a cover with a fitted base, remember to add 6in to the length measurements of the chair sides, front and back. For rectangular cushions, measure the top, base and sides and add on the seam allowance. For shaped cushions, measure the top and base at the widest parts and cut out rectangles; these can be trimmed to fit the cushion when pinned together.

Calculating the fabric

Each chair or sofa must be measured and fabric requirements calculated individually. However, as a rough indication of quantities, using 48in-wide fabric, a three-piece suite needs about 24yd, a three-seater sofa 11yd and an armchair about 7¾yd. After measuring the chair, check the measurements and the appropriate allowances for seams, tuck-in and turn-under at the base. In addition, if required, include the measurements for cushions and a skirt.

☐ Next make a layout chart. Draw this to scale, ⅛in = 1in, on graph paper. On the graph paper draw an elongated rectangle with the width to the measurement of the fabric, for example 6in for 48in wide fabric. If patterned fabric has been chosen, mark the fabric repeat to scale along the entire drawn length of the fabric.

☐ On a separate sheet of plain paper draw and cut out your pattern pieces to the same scale. On each mark the direction of the grain, following the guide lines (fig. 6). Also mark the top and what it represents. Position the pattern pieces on the graph paper layout and move them around to get the most economical layout (fig. 7). On the layout, ensure that the grain lines run in the same direction and that the design motifs are positioned centrally. Allow the fabric for the piping, if the seams are to be piped.

☐ Pin all the pieces in place and measure the length of the layout. Convert the measurement back to inches and then to yards. This is the amount of fabric you should buy, but be generous when estimating the fabric. Leftover fabric can always be used for matching throw pillows or for protective arm covers. Keep the layout as a cutting guide.

Cutting out the fabric

☐ Check that your paper layout is accurate before cutting out the fabric pieces. If you are working with a large fabric design, double-check that it will appear in the center of the cushions and, when joining fabric widths to cover the sofa back, make sure that the design of the fabric matches exactly across the seams.

☐ Remember to cut out only simple rectangles. These rectangles will be cut piece by piece as they are fitted piece by piece onto the chair. As each piece is cut out, mark the top on each one and what part of the chair it will cover.

Fitting

☐ Mark a center line with pins or tailor's chalk down the center back of the chair and its seat (fig. 8). Using large, brightly-colored basting stitches, mark the center line on each fabric piece along the straight grain. This helps to keep the fabric absolutely straight and gives the cover a better fit.

☐ The cover is put together inside out on the chair. Work methodically, always pinning, trimming, basting and then stitching.

☐ Begin by placing the inside back panel in position on the chair, matching the basted line on the cover to the pins on the chair and keeping the fabric straight. Smooth out any wrinkles. Pin the inside back panel to the chair to hold it firmly in place (fig. 9).

☐ Repeat with the outside back panel, pinning it to the inside back panel along the top seamline. If this seam is curved, the fabric will have to be eased or small darts made to achieve a smooth fit. Trim off any excess fabric to within ¾in of the fitting line as it has been pinned in place.

☐ Place the seat cover in position with the small seam allowance at the front and the larger tuck-in allowance at the sides and back; fold the tuck-in allow-

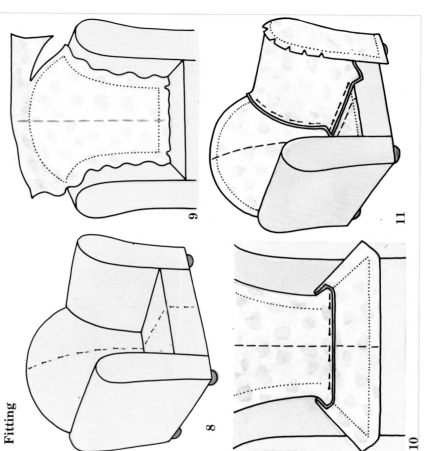

Fitting

9

8

11

10

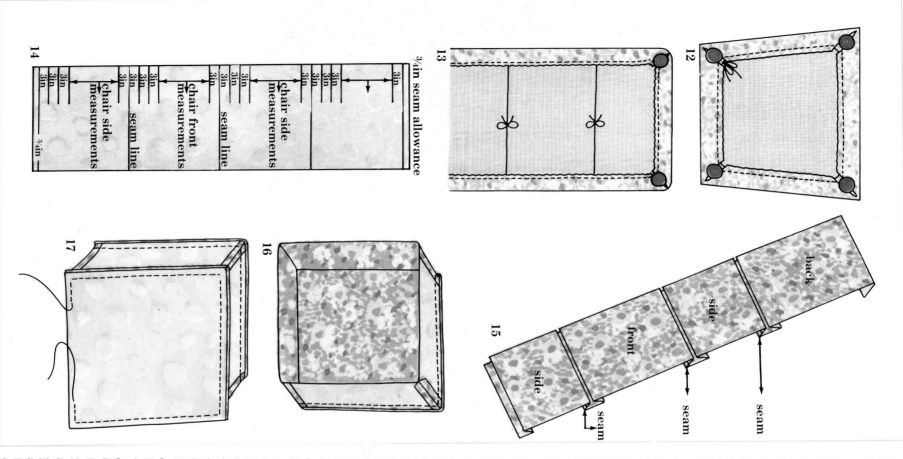

ance back on itself. Pin the inside back panel and seat cover together along the tuck-in allowance (fig. 10).

☐ Place the inside, top and outside arm pieces over one chair arm and pin to each other to fit. The outside arm should also be fitted to the outside back panel and the inside arm to the inside back panel and seat cover. Allow for the tuck-in around seat. Fit the front arm piece. If the seams follow a curve, clip the seam allowance (fig. 11). Repeat and fit the other arm.

☐ Fit the front seat. Depending on the chair design, this piece can be awkward because the side seams at the top may need to be seamed to the tuck-in at the side of the seat while lower down they are seamed to the front arm piece.

☐ If the cover is to have a skirt, leave the fitting of this until the major part of the cover is completed.

☐ If the cover is to be piped, take extra care that the fitting lines (future seamlines) are clearly marked with either pins or tailor's chalk. Notch the seam allowances so that the pieces can be matched together again easily.

☐ To insert the piping, remove the cover from the chair. Unpin each seam, a little at a time, insert the covered piping cord and re-pin the seam. If the cover is not piped, the pieces need not be taken apart.

☐ Baste and stitch any fitting darts. Baste the cover together. Turn the cover right side out. Place the cover, right side out, over the chair. Check the fit of the cover on the chair and make any final adjustments. Remove from chair. Stitch together, leaving a seam at the back corner open.

Finishing the base

Fitted base – a slip cover fitted along the lower edge is held in place under the chair by a drawstring of cotton tape. Measure around the lower edge of the chair for the correct tape length.

☐ Unpick the base seams to within ⅜in of chair bottom.

☐ With cover in place, turn the chair upside down. Pin the fabric around the casters at each of the four corners (fig. 12).

☐ Make a 1in double casing hem to finish the lower edge of the four flaps and to carry the drawstring; pin in place. Remove the cover; baste and stitch each casing hem in place.

☐ Starting at the opening corner, thread the drawstring tape through

each casing in turn. Place the cover over the chair. Pull up the drawstring tape to fit and tie the ends together (fig. 12). Do not cut off the excess tape, as the fullness is needed when the cover is removed for cleaning. Tuck the ends up under one of the hems.

☐ If the chair is large or if you are covering a sofa, a combination of a casing tape and tapes tied across the base width is best. Simply cut two tapes the width of the sofa for each tie. Stitch in place under the hem at opposite sides of the cover. Space the ties at 12in intervals along the length of cover (fig. 13).

Box pleated skirt base – a pleated skirt base will produce an elegant tailored effect.

☐ Fit the cover on the chair. Measuring from the floor, mark seamline for skirt. If the seam is to be piped, baste the covered piping cord in position. Pin, baste and stitch the four skirt strips together into one long strip.

☐ Measure off 3in for pleats on either side of each seam (fig. 14). In this way all the seams will be completely hidden.

☐ Pleat the fabric following the marks (fig. 15). Baste along the top of the skirt to hold the pleats in place.

☐ Remove the cover from the chair. Pin and baste the skirt in place, starting at the open corner.

☐ Replace the cover on the chair; check the fit and mark the hemline. Remove the cover. Stitch the skirt to the cover. Turn up a double hem; baste and hand stitch in place.

The opening

The opening down one of the side back seams needs to be finished as neatly as possible and is always left until last to achieve a good fit.

☐ Bind the two opening edges with 3in wide strips of matching fabric, to neaten them.

☐ Fasten the opening with hooks and eyes or strips of Velcro®, insert a zipper or simply stitch the opening closed by hand when the cover is completely finished, although this will make it more difficult to remove the covers.

Finishing the cover

☐ Trim off any excess seam allowance and press all the seams open. Press the cover well and fit onto the chair. Give the cover a final press after fitting.

☐ When replacing the cover after washing, put the cover, still damp, on the chair and press for a good fit.

Cushions

☐ Pin, baste and stitch the ends of the cushion side piece (cushion gusset) together into a ring.

☐ With right sides together, pin, baste and stitch cushion side piece to all four sides of one cushion piece, taking a ¾in seam allowance (fig. 16). If the cushions are to be trimmed with pipings, insert covered piping cord in between side and cover pieces.

☐ Match second cushion piece to opposite long edge of side piece with right sides together, inserting piping if used.

Pin and baste. Stitch together, starting 2in in from one corner on one side and ending 2in along at the opposite end of the first side (fig. 17). Clip the corners and the seam allowances. When this has been done, turn the cushion cover so that it is right side out.

☐ Finish the opening as you did for the main cover. Now, simply fit it carefully over the cushion.

Note *If the cushions are shaped, pin and fit the covers carefully over the cushions in exactly the same way as you did for the main cover.*

Simple Sofa

This easy-to-make sofa is constructed around two mattresses. Use two old but firm ones or buy two blocks of solid foam in the correct size. Either way the result will be comfortable and a lasting success.

Finished size
75in long, 26½in deep, 26in high

Materials
Two mattresses or pieces of foam 75 × 26½in, 7½in thick
10yd of 60in-wide upholstery grade pinwale corduroy
Styrofoam granules for filling arms and back
5½yd of 45in-wide muslin

Six pieces of medium-weight iron-on canvas for arm ends
Two pieces of cardboard 16½ × 10¼in for arm bases
One piece of cardboard 75 × 10¼in for back base
6½yd of ⅝in-wide gripper tape
Matching sewing thread
Paper for pattern

☐ Make a paper pattern for the arm/back ends. On a piece of paper draw a rectangle 12½in high by 12in wide. Mark a point 4¾in in from one corner on both top and side edges. Draw a curve from point to point (fig 1). Cut along the marked curve. Fold the pattern in half from top to bottom and mark the opposite corner in the same way. Round off the second corner to match.

☐ Cut out all the fabric pieces following the cutting layout for measurements.
☐ Cut out six arm/back ends from iron-on canvas. Position the shiny side to the wrong side of each fabric end. Press in place.
☐ Place two mattress side pieces with right sides together, matching all edges. Pin, baste and stitch one short edge (fig.2). Repeat with two more mattress side pieces.

45

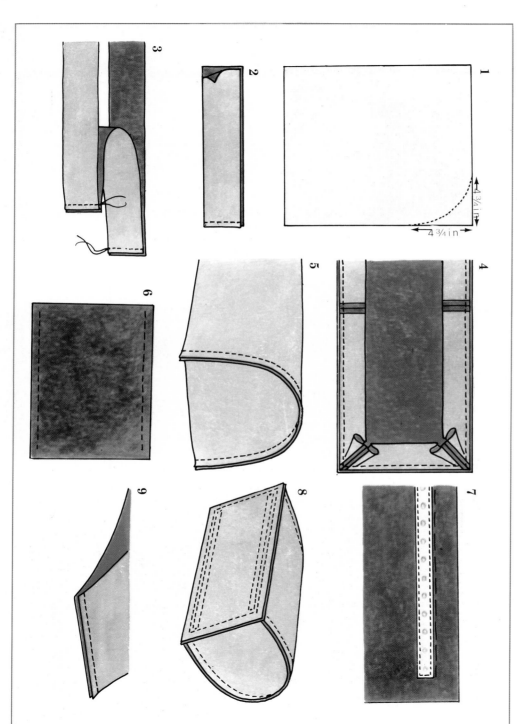

☐Position one mattress side end piece between the two joined side pieces with right sides together and short edges matching. Pin, baste and stitch short edges (fig. 3). Do the same with second side end piece to form the complete side piece in the shape of a ring.

☐Position the complete side piece on one main mattress piece with right sides together. Place the end seams at the corners of main piece and the seams in the side pieces in the center of each long side of main piece. Ensure that the pile on the side piece is running upward. Pin, baste and stitch together all around the outer edge (fig. 4).

☐Repeat; pin and baste the second main mattress piece to the opposite edge of side piece in the same way for the base. Stitch together all around, leaving one short edge and 19½in down both long sides open for insertion of the mattress.

☐Trim and turn mattress cover right side out. Insert one mattress inside the cover. Pin the opening edges together to close temporarily.

☐Make the second mattress cover in the same way.

☐With the pile running upward from the inner arm, position the long edge of one piece to the curved edge of one arm end, with right sides together and easing the fabric evenly around the curve. Pin, baste and stitch in place (fig. 5). Repeat with the second arm end at the opposite end of the arm piece.

☐Mark a line with basting stitches on long edges of one arm base, 1½in from the outer edges (fig. 6).

☐Cut two lengths of gripper tape to fit the long edges of the arm base on the marked lines. Position the top half of each length of gripper tape in position on arm base with outer edges butting up against the basted lines; turn under the ends neatly. Pin, baste and stitch the gripper tape in place down all sides of each piece (fig. 7). Keep the opposite lengths of tape handy as they will be stitched to one of the mattress covers.

☐Position arm base on arm piece with right sides together. Pin, baste and stitch together, leaving the seam open at base of back end (fig. 8). Trim seams and turn arm right side out. Trim down iron-on canvas close to seamline.

☐Cut out arm and back pieces from muslin following the cutting layout for measurements.

☐Make another arm in muslin for the lining, leaving the seam open at base of back end. Trim seams and turn lining arm right side out.

☐Place the muslin arm inside the corduroy arm with right side of muslin to wrong side of corduroy, matching all seams.

☐Place one of the cardboard bases inside the muslin arm. Fill the muslin arm firmly with styrofoam granules. Turn in the opening edges on muslin arm and slipstitch firmly together to close. Turn in opening edges on the corduroy arm and slipstitch firmly together to close.

☐Make the second arm piece in the same way, but reverse the direction of the pile so that it will still run from the inner arm to the outer arm.

☐Place the corduroy back pieces with

Cutting layout

¾in seam allowance included.

Key to layout for 60in-wide fabric
A Mattress
B Mattress side ends
C Mattress sides
D Arm/back ends
E Backs
F Back base
G Arms
H Arm bases

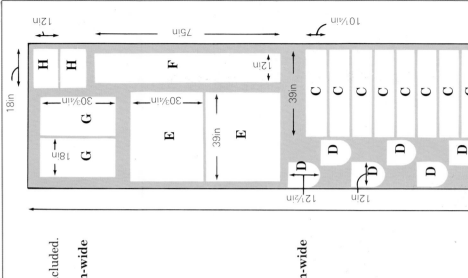

Key to layout for 45in-wide fabric
D Arm/back ends
E Backs
F Back base
G Arms
H Arm bases

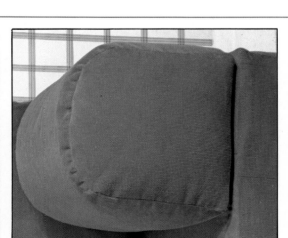

right sides together, matching all edges. Pin, baste and stitch one short edge for center back seam (fig. 9). Repeat with muslin back pieces.

☐Make the back in the same way as the arms, with pile running upward from the inside back.

☐Position the back and arms on top of one mattress cover, butting the outer edges together. Mark the positions of the lengths of gripper on the mattress cover.

☐Remove the mattress from the cover. Position the opposite halves of each length of gripper on the mattress cover at the sides and back edge, matching all the marks. Pin, baste and stitch each length in position on all sides of each piece (fig. 10).

☐Replace the cover over the mattress. Turn in the opening edges on the cover. Slipstitch the edges firmly together to close. Slipstitch the opening edges together on the second mattress cover.

☐Position top mattress on top of second mattress, matching all edges. Fasten back and then both arms in place.

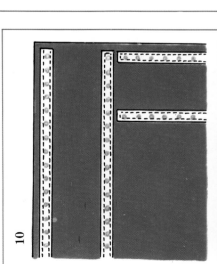

10

Chair Bed

This comfortable quilted seat is easy and economical to make and quickly and cleverly converts into a single bed.

Finished size
Approx. 36 × 30in, 14in deep
Materials
6½yd of 48in-wide upholstery linen
6½yd of 45in-wide cotton fabric for backing
14½yd of 36in-wide lightweight batting

Two foam cushions 35½ × 29½in and 7in thick
Foam chips for headrest
Matching and contrasting sewing thread
Paper for pattern
Tailor's chalk

□ Make a paper pattern for the headrest side: on a sheet of paper draw a rectangle 12½ × 11in. Mark a point along one long edge 5in from corner. Mark a point from the same corner, 1½in along short edge. Join together with a curved line, with the point on long edge as the top of the curve. Continue the line, cutting off next corner to opposite corner on second long edge. Cut out the resulting pattern (fig. 1).

□ Cut out all the pieces from upholstery fabric following the cutting layout below. In the same way, cut out all the pieces from backing cotton.

□ Using backing fabric pieces as patterns, cut the gussets and headrest sides from a single thickness of batting and the other pieces from double thickness.

□ Place all three main pieces together, with the batting sandwiched between the fabric and the backing fabric. Pin and baste together all around (fig. 2).

□ Repeat for the other pieces.

□ Mark quilting lines on the main fabric piece using tailor's chalk. On the right side, mark the lines 6in apart across the width and down the length of the fabric. Mark the first line 6¾in from the raw edges (fig. 3).

□ Baste along each quilting line. Using a larger-than-average stitch, work along each basted line using a contrasting sewing thread. Do not stitch the marked center line across the fabric width (fig. 4). Repeat with cushion base, stitching all the quilting lines. Repeat on the seat top, but begin the widthwise lines 2¾in from one short edge. Mark, but do not stitch the next widthwise line.

□ Position the main piece to the marked line of the seat top. Place with wrong sides together and with center line of main piece to marked, unstitched widthwise quilting line, 8½in from short edge on seat top.

□ Turn in ¾in at the side edges of both pieces. Pin, baste and stitch together through all thicknesses on the marked quilting line, using contrasting sewing thread (fig. 5).

□ Mark and stitch the quilting lines on headrest: begin the quilting lines 6¾in from one long edge and end 3in from opposite long edge.

□ Position one headrest side piece to headrest top. Place with right sides and short edges together and with the 6¾in quilted edge to slope at front. Pin, baste and stitch together (fig. 6).

□ Repeat, stitching second headrest side piece in position

Cutting layouts
¾in seam allowance included

Key to layout

A Main piece	**D** Cushion base
B Gusset	**E** Headrest
C Seat top	**F** Headrest side

48/50in-wide fabric

(Layout diagram: pieces A, C, D, E with B, B across the top; F, F curved pieces. Dimensions: 72½in, 63¾in, 37in, 27½in; 31in between quilting sections; 101in; 8½in, 8½in; 48in wide; 6⅛yd.)

45in-wide fabric

(Layout diagram: pieces A, C, D, E with B, B; F, F curved pieces. Dimensions: 11in, 12½in; 45in wide; 6⅛yd.)

□Position complete headrest to seat top with end of headrest to end of seat top and headrest sides to side of seat top. Pin, baste and stitch in place (fig. 7). Turn headrest right side out. Leave the back seam open for filling.

□Position one short edge of cushion base to opposite end of seat top. Pin, baste and stitch together.

□Clip the seam allowance on both sides of the center quilted line on the main section ⅜in from the stitching line. Position one long edge of one gus-

set to one half of main piece. Pin one short end of gusset to center of main piece. Continue pinning down the side, along the end up to opposite side of center. Baste and stitch in place, starting and ending at clip mark in seam allowances (fig. 8). Repeat, stitching the second gusset in place to opposite half of main piece.

□On one side, pin, baste and stitch gusset end to seat top (fig. 9). Continue, stitching remaining long gusset edge to seat top, leaving back seam open.

□Pin, baste and stitch remaining long edge of second gusset to lower front of cushion base, leaving the back seam open for filling.

□Trim; turn cover right side out. Insert a piece of foam into each cushion section. Turn in the opening edges for ¾in on cushion base. Stitch edges firmly together to close. Fill headrest with foam chips. Turn in ¾in on top gusset. Pin, baste and stitch together by hand to close opening (fig. 11).

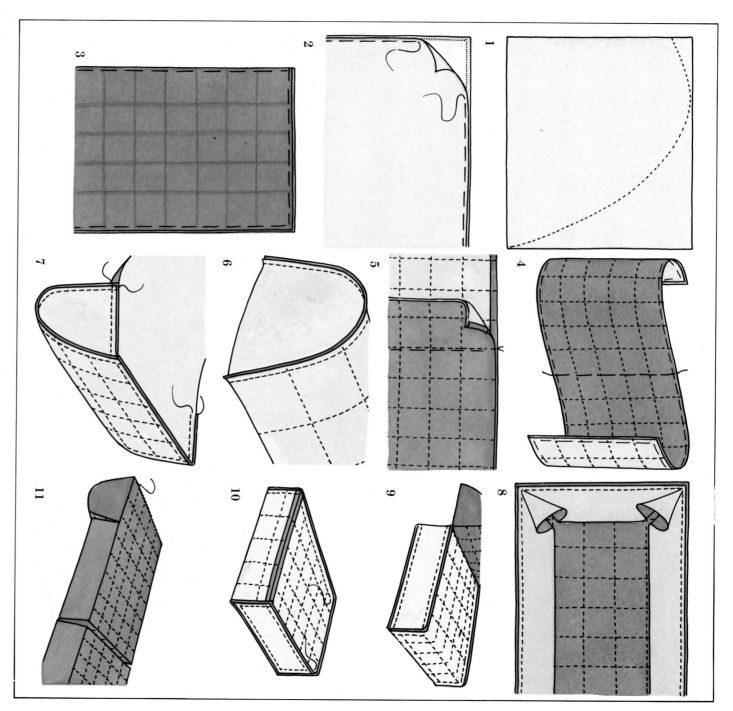

Kitchen Chair Seats

Make your kitchen seating that little bit more comfortable – and attractive – with easy-to-make chair cushions. They fasten to standard wooden chair backs with toggles.

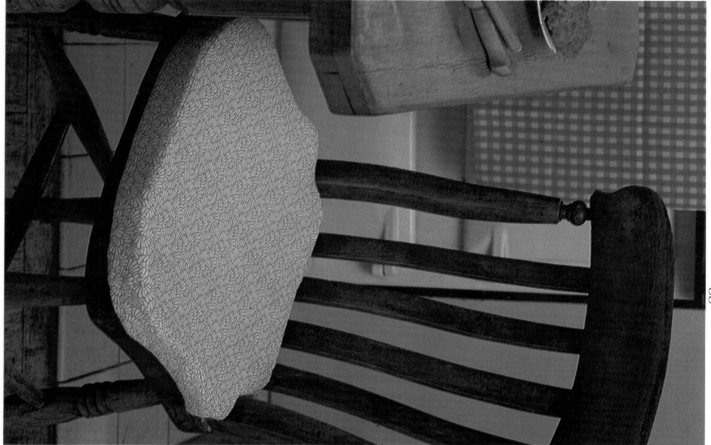

Finished size
As measured

Materials (for 4 cushions)
Tracing paper and white paper
3yd of 48in-wide furnishing cotton
Four pieces of 1½in-thick foam,
16in square
Eight toggles
1yd of ¼in-wide elastic
Machine sewing thread
Sharp kitchen knife

□ Make a pattern of the chair seat. Lay a sheet of tracing paper across the chair seat and mark the front and side edges of the seat. Mark the shape in front of the struts at the back of the chair, so the cushion will fit snugly. Mark the positions of the outer struts of the seat back to which cushion will be fastened (fig. 1).

□ Remove the paper and cut out around the marked pattern. Fold the pattern in half lengthwise to check that it is even. Place the pattern on a sheet of white paper and mark around it. Add ⅝in all around the pattern for the seam allowance (fig. 2). Mark the fastening strut positions on the pattern. Mark the center back and center front of cushion.

□ From fabric cut out eight cushion pieces. Mark the fastening struts and center back and front on each cushion piece.

□ For length of gusset, measure around the pattern along seamline and add 1in to this measurement for seam allowance. Cut out four 2¾in-wide gusset pieces on the bias of the fabric.

□ For fastening straps, cut out a strip of fabric 63in long and 1½in wide on the bias of the fabric. Fold the bias strip in half lengthwise. Pin, baste and stitch down the length, ⅜in from the edges (fig. 3). Trim. Turn strip right side out.

□ For each toggle fastening strip, from the bias strip cut a piece 2in long. For each loop fastening, from bias strip cut out a piece 5½in long. Cut out eight pieces of elastic each 4in long for loop fastenings. (Make eight sets in all.)

□ Thread one piece of elastic through one loop fastening strip, securing the elastic to fabric at both ends (fig. 4).

□ Fold the loop in half, matching short edges together. Pin and baste raw edges of loop to one inside strut position on back edge of one cushion piece. Position the loop on the right side of the cushion piece, facing inward (fig. 5).

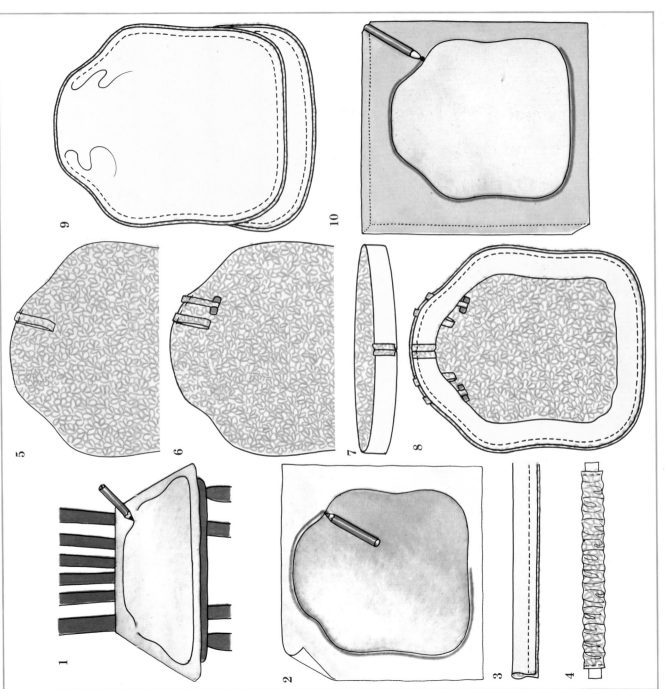

□ Turn in short edges for ³⁄₈in on one toggle fastening strip. Slipstitch edges together to close for toggle end of fastening strip. Pin and baste raw edges of toggle fastening strip to one outside strut position on back edge of cushion piece. Place fastening strip to one side of cushion piece, facing inward (fig. 6). (Toggles are attached later.)

□ Repeat; pin and baste second pair of fastenings to back of cushion piece on the opposite side to the first pair.

□ Pin, baste and stitch one gusset piece together into a ring. Place with right sides together, taking ⁵⁄₈in seam allowance (fig. 7).

□ Position one long edge of gusset to cushion piece with fastenings. Place the gusset and cushion piece with right sides together and with gusset seam to center back of cushion. Pin gusset in position, easing around the corners. Baste and stitch in place all around, catching in the fastenings (fig. 8). Trim the seam allowance and clip into the curves so the gusset will fit neatly around the curved edges.

□ Pin second cushion piece to opposite long edge of gusset, matching centers. Position with right sides together. Pin, baste and stitch in place, leaving a 7in opening at the back of the cushion

(fig. 9). Trim seam allowance and clip curves. Turn cushion right side out.

□ Stitch a toggle to the end of each toggle fastening strip.

□ Trim seam allowance off the paper pattern. Position the trimmed pattern on one piece of foam. Mark around it with a ball-point pen. Using a kitchen knife or large scissors, cut the foam to the correct shape, following the marked line.

□ Insert the foam into the cushion cover. Turn in the opening edges. Slip-stitch the edges together to close.

□ Make three more cushions in the same way.

53

Sag Bag

These colorful sag bags are not only as comfortable as they look, but also inexpensive and a cinch to make!

Materials
4yd of 48in-wide patterned fabric
4yd of 48in-wide lining
A total of ½ cubic yard of styrofoam granules
Matching thread

(⅝ seam allowance is included.)

Note We chose heavyweight cottons for our sag bags, but they can be made in a variety of fabrics, which include thick jersey knits, woolens, pinwale corduroy or synthetic leather or suede. To make them even more colorful, alternate the colors of the sides, top and base – this is also a good way to use up odd yard lengths of fabric. The top and bottom sections together take less than 1yd of fabric.

It is possible to cut two side pieces from 1yd of fabric.
□ Make a paper pattern for the top. Draw a vertical line 19in long. Draw a horizontal line through the center of the vertical line, 22in long. At each end of vertical line draw horizontal lines, parallel to center line, each 5½in long (fig. 1). Join the top of the long horizontal line to the top of the short horizontal lines. Repeat for bottom points to form a hexagon (fig. 2).
□ Make a paper pattern for the base, in

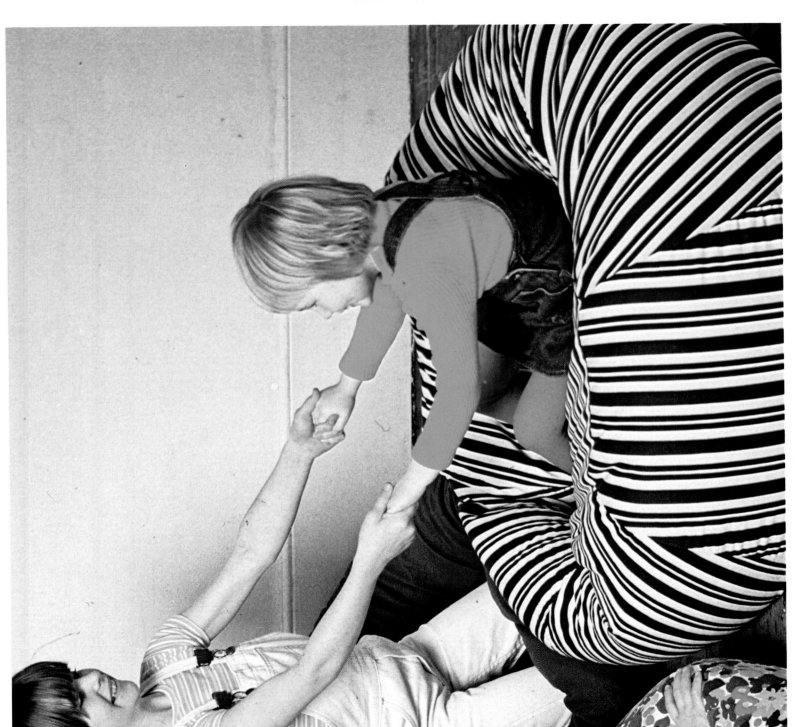

the same way, but make main vertical line 25in long, main horizontal line right sides facing. Pin, baste and stitch 28½in long and horizontal lines at each end 7in long.

☐ Make pattern for side section. Draw a vertical line 36in long. Draw a horizontal line through the center 23in long. At one end draw a horizontal line 11in long for the top and at opposite end draw a horizontal line 14in long for the base. Join outer points of top and base through outer point on center line. Draw this freehand to gain a curved shape. Repeat on opposite side (fig. 3).

☐ From patterned fabric cut one top, one base and six side sections.

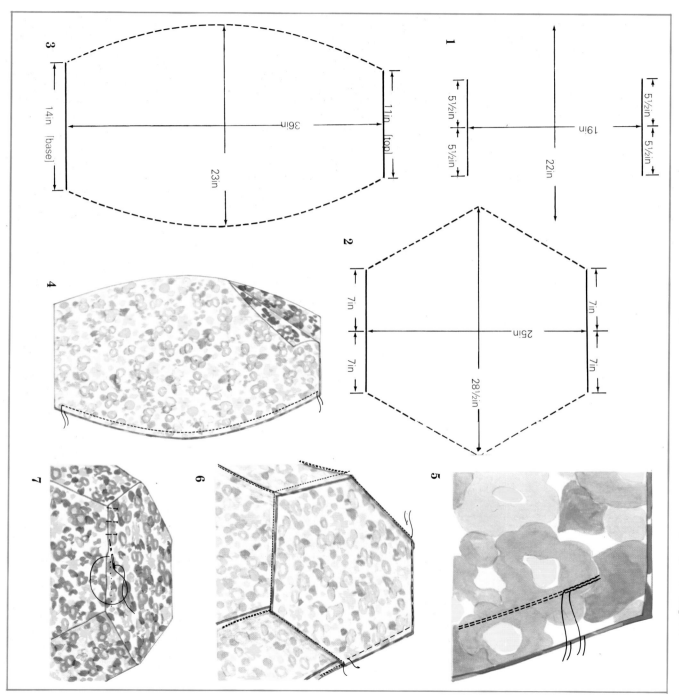

1

5½in ←→ 5½in

19in

22in

2

7in

25in

7in

7in

7in

28½in

3

14in [base]

11in [top]

36in

23in

4

5

6

7

☐ Place two side sections together, right sides facing. Pin, baste and stitch in place in the same way, but leave two sides open. When this has been done, turn sag bag right side out.

☐ Make the lining in the same way but leave only one side open.

☐ Using a bowl as a scoop, fill the lining with granules. The granules will not fill the bag completely; this allows room for them to move when someone sits on the bag. Turn in opening edges of lining and overcast them firmly together.

☐ Push filled lining inside outer covers. Turn in opening edges and slipstitch them firmly together (fig. 7).

along one side edge to within ½in of sides open. When this has been done, each end (fig. 4). Stitch down seam turn sag bag right side out. allowance and ☐ Make the lining in the same way but close to the first row of stitching, for leave only one side open. added strength (fig. 5). Repeat, stitch- ing all the side sections together in exactly the same way so that, when you with granules. The granules will not have finished, a ring is formed.

☐ Leave the bag wrong side out. Place the top section, wrong side up, over the smaller opening, and pin it in place, matching raw edges and with right sides facing and aligning side seams with corner points. Stitch the seam

twice, as before (fig. 6). Stitch the base in place in the same way, but leave two

Bolsters

There is seemingly no end to the versatility of the bolster cushion. You can make an attractive floor cushion, add style and comfort to your living room sofa or add a perfect finishing touch to a pretty bedroom setting.

Floor pillow

Finished size

About 90in long and 16in in diameter; ¾in seam allowance is included

Materials

3⅛yd of 48/50in-wide fabric
2⅝yd of 90in-wide sheeting
Paper for pattern
Styrofoam granules for filling
Matching sewing thread

☐ Make a paper pattern for a 16½in diameter circle. Fold a 20in-square piece of paper evenly into quarters. On this folded piece of paper draw a quarter circle, using string and a pencil. Fasten one end of the string around a thumb tack. Tie the opposite end of the string around the pencil with the string 8¼in long. Fasten the thumb tack into the folded corner of the paper. Keeping the string taut, draw an arc from corner to corner (fig. 1). Keeping the paper folded, cut along the marked line. Unfold the paper pattern.

☐ For bolster pad, using the pattern cut out two end circles from lining fabric. Cut out one piece 91½ × 48in for main bolster section. Fold main lining bolster section in half lengthwise with right sides together, edges even. Pin, baste and stitch long edges together, leaving a 30in opening in the center of the seam (fig. 2).

☐ Position one lining end circle to one end of main section. Place with right sides together, matching edges. Pin, baste and stitch in position. Snip into seam allowance (fig. 3).

☐ Repeat at opposite end of the main piece. Trim and turn bolster pad right side out.

☐ Fill the bolster pad with styrofoam granules. Do not overfill, so the bolster will be able to bend into different shapes. Turn in opening edges. Slipstitch the folded edges firmly together to close.

□Make the outer cover for the bolster following exactly the same method as you used for the inner one.

□Insert the bolster pad into the bolster cover (fig. 4). Turn in the folded edges. Slipstitch the folded edges neatly together.

Floor pillow

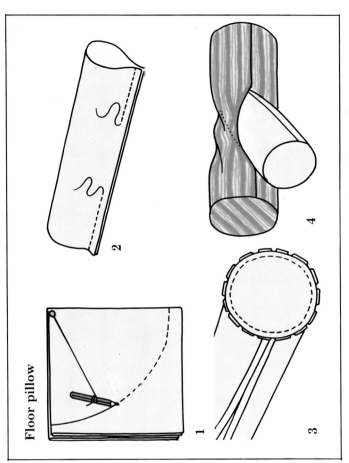

Sofa bolsters

Finished size

About 21½in long and 8in in diameter; ¾in seam allowance is included

Materials (for each bolster)

½yd of 48in-wide dark print fabric
½yd of 48in-wide light print fabric
½yd of 36in-wide plain fabric
3yd of piping cord
1yd of 36in-wide lining fabric
Paper for patterns
Fiberfill for stuffing
Matching sewing thread

□To make the pattern for the bolster end circle, make a paper pattern as for floor bolster cushion, but with the string only 4½in long.

□From dark print fabric cut out two end circles. Cut out one piece 26½ × 7½in for middle section.

□From light print fabric cut out two pieces each 26½ × 9½in for outer sections.

□From solid color fabric make a length of piping: cut out 2in-wide strips on bias of fabric. Pin, baste and stitch strips together, making a 3yd length, the same length as piping cord (fig. 1).

□Fold the piping fabric around the piping cord with wrong side inside. Pin and baste down the complete length, close to the piping cord, to hold it firmly in place (fig. 2).

□Fold one outer section piece in half widthwise, with right sides together and edges even. Pin, baste and stitch seam.

□Stitch the second outer section piece into a ring in the same way.

□Fold center section piece in half widthwise, with right sides together, matching edges. Pin, baste and stitch ¾in from each side, leaving center of seam open (fig. 3). Turn right side out.

□Pin the covered piping cord to both raw edges of the center bolster section. Position the covered piping cord, starting at the seam with the piping facing inward. Cut off the excess piping cord and stitch the piping fabric together to fit. Baste the covered piping cord firmly in position (fig. 4).

□Pin more covered piping cord around one end circle. Position the cord facing inward and snip into the seam allowance to ease it around the circle. Cut off excess piping cord and stitch the piping fabric together to fit. Baste the covered piping cord so that it is firmly in position (fig. 5).

□Repeat with second fabric end circle.

□Position one outer bolster section on one piped edge of center section. Place with seams and edges matching and with right sides together. Pin, baste and stitch in place. Repeat with second outer bolster section.

Place one piped end circle to one end of bolster piece. Position with right sides together, matching seams and edges. Pin, baste and stitch in position. Repeat with second end circle piece. Trim and turn the bolster cover right side out.

□To make the bolster pad: from lining

Sofa bolsters

fabric cut out two end circles and one piece 26½ × 23¼in. Fold lining main piece in half lengthwise. Fold lining main piece in half lengthwise with right sides together, matching edges. Pin, baste and stitch the long edges, making sure that you have left an opening in the center of the seam.

□Stitch end circle to one end of the bolster pad, as for cover. Repeat, stitching the second end circle in place. Trim and turn bolster pad so that it is right side out.

□Insert filling into bolster pad. Turn in opening edges. Slipstitch folded edges together firmly to close.

□Insert bolster pad into outer cover. Turn in opening edges. Slipstitch folded edges neatly together to close (fig. 6).

□Make second bolster in the same way as the first one.

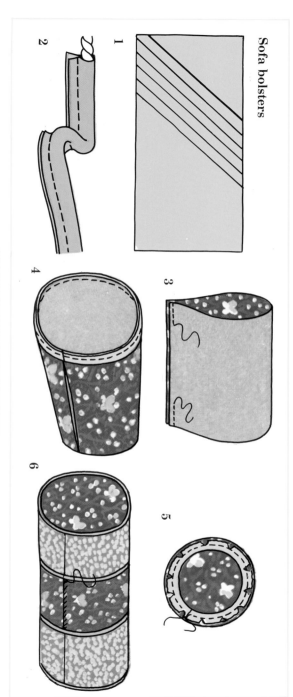

Bedroom bolsters

Finished size

About 18in long and 6¾in in diameter; ¾in seam allowance is included

Materials (for each bolster)
1½yd of 45in-wide satin
One bolster pad 18in long, 6¾in in diameter
Two 7in tassels
Matching sewing thread

□From satin cut out one piece 22¾ × 26¾in. Fold satin in half lengthwise, with right sides together and edges even. Pin, baste and stitch long edges, taking ¾in seam allowance (fig. 1). Turn right side out.

□Turn in raw edges at each end for ¾in. Pin and baste. Run a line of gathering stitches close to folded edge at one end, leaving the gathering thread hanging free (fig. 2). Repeat this whole procedure at the opposite end of the cover.

□Insert the bolster pad into cover. Pull up gathering thread at each end and fasten off (fig. 3).

□Position the rosette of one tassel over gathered end of bolster. Slipstitch in place by hand, covering gathered end (fig. 4). Repeat at opposite end of bolster.

□Make second bolster in the same way as the first one.

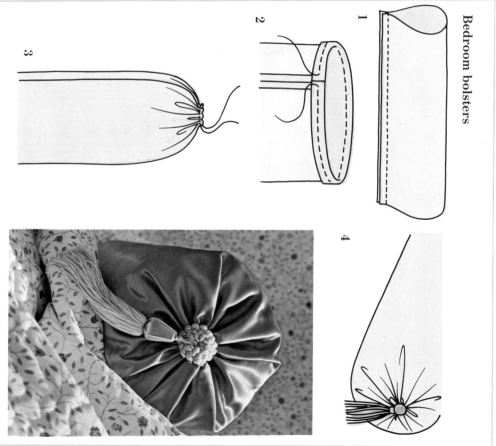

Appliqué Pillows

Machine or hand appliqué is an easy way to make an ordinary pillow into something very special.

Finished size
16in square
Materials (for 1 pillow)
½yd of 36in-wide solid color fabric
16in square of printed cotton for border
Scraps of plain and printed cottons for motifs
Iron-on interfacing
Matching sewing thread
16in-square cushion form
10in zipper (optional)
Dressmaker's carbon paper

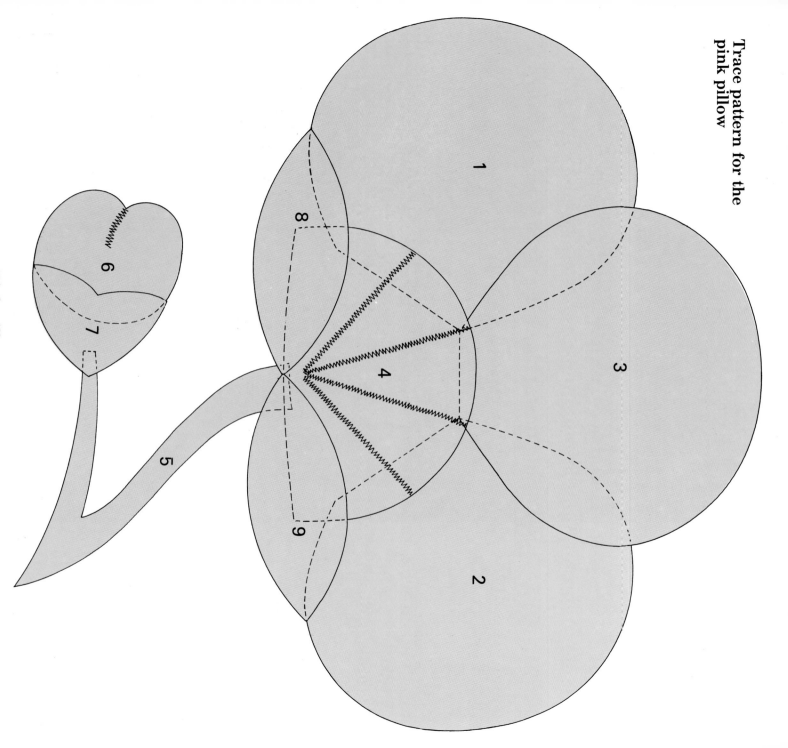

Trace pattern for the pink pillow

Note *The numbers represent the order in which the pieces should be applied. The dotted lines indicate the areas where pieces overlap. Zig-zag lines indicate machine zig-zag embroidery.*

Pink pillow

☐ Trace the motifs from the trace pattern and transfer them onto the iron-on interfacing with the carbon paper. Draw a border, 1½in wide and 13in long on the outside, on the interfacing. Cut out motifs and border, leaving an extra ¼in around all edges (fig. 1). The dotted lines on the diagram indicate where parts of the design overlap.

☐ Iron each motif and the border onto the back of the appropriate fabric. Allow them to cool, then cut out accurately around each shape, trimming off the ¼in border (fig. 2).

☐ Cut out two 18in squares from the pink fabric for back and front of pillow.

☐ With right sides upward, position border on pillow front with outer edge

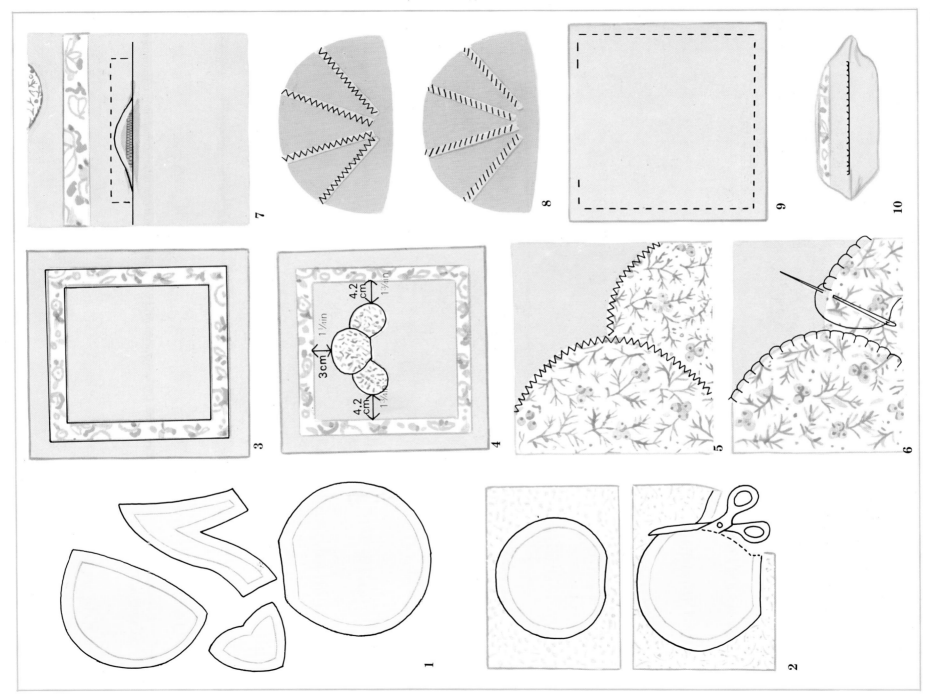

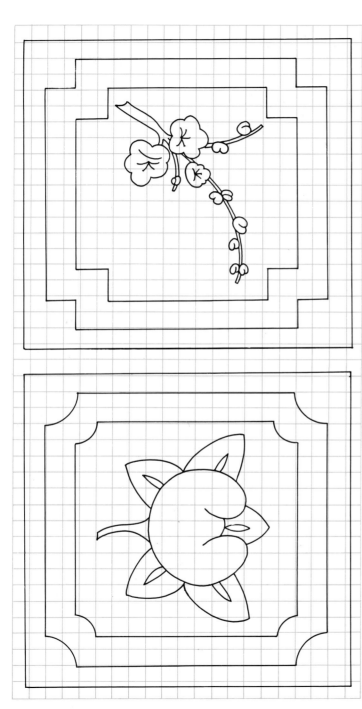

Designs for green pillow

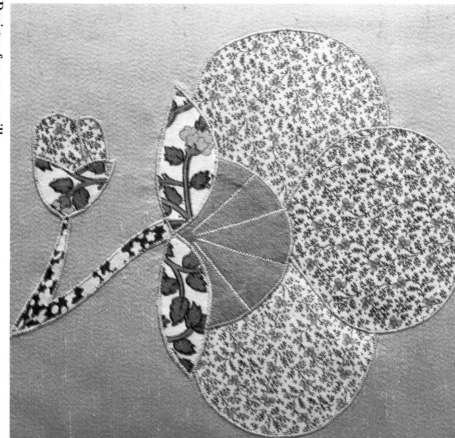

of border 2in from raw edges. Secure with basting if pieces are backed with iron-on interfacing, or iron on in position if using fusible interfacing (fig. 3).

□ Position the cut-out flower pieces in the order which is indicated on the pattern in the center of the border design (fig. 4).

□ Using matching thread stitch around the edge of each appliqué piece using close machine zig-zag stitch (fig. 5). Use blanket stitch if you are working by hand (fig. 6).

□ Machine embroider where indicated, using either zig-zag or satin stitch.

□ If using a zipper, insert this into one side seam before making the pillow (fig. 8).

□ Place pillow back on pillow front, with right sides together, and raw edges even. Stitch together, taking 1in seams and leaving a 10in opening for turning right side out (fig. 9).

□ Turn pillow cover right side out. Insert pillow form and slipstitch the opening together, if you have not fitted a zipper (fig. 10).

Green pillows

These pillows are made in the same way as the pink pillows, using the same materials.

□ Enlarge one or both of the designs given on this page. Each of the small squares represents a square measuring ¾in on a side. Take a sheet of paper and, using a ruler, draw a grid of ¾in squares, 21 across and 21 down. Copy the designs on your enlarged grid, positioning each part of the drawing on the square corresponding to the equivalent square on the small grid.

□ Trace the enlarged design motifs and proceed as for the pink pillow.

Lace Pillows

These exquisite lace-trimmed pillows are ideal for a romantic bedroom.

Pillow with square trim

Finished size

16in square

Materials

½yd of 36in-wide white linen
8½in square of pale pink fabric
8½in square of white lace fabric
2yd of ⅜in-wide pale pink ribbon
¾yd of ¾in-wide white edging lace
1¼yd of 1in-wide eyelet edging
Scrap of white polka-dot cotton fabric
16in-square pillow form
Pink and white thread

☐ From white fabric cut out two pieces, each 17¼in square. Mark the center of one square – the front – by folding the fabric diagonally in half twice. Mark the center of the pink fabric square in the same way (fig. 1).

☐ Place the pink fabric square, right side up, diagonally over the right side of the front piece, matching centers. Pin in place around edges (fig. 2).

☐ Place the white lace square centrally over the pink fabric square and baste in place through all three layers (fig. 3).

☐ Pin and baste the eyelet edging, right side up, around the edge of the lace-covered square, just overlapping the fabric edges, mitering the corners. Turn in the ends at one corner and slipstich them together (fig. 4).

☐ Pin and baste the pink ribbon along all sides of the lace-covered square, overlapping the edge of the eyelet edging. Miter the corners and turn in the ends as on eyelet edging. Topstitch or zig-zag stitch along edges (fig.5).

☐ Cut the polka-dot fabric into four right-angled triangles with two equal sides of 6in. Place one triangle, right side up, over each corner of pillow front. Pin and baste in place (fig. 6).

☐ Cut the edging lace into four equal lengths. Baste each length, right side up, along the long edge of each corner triangle, with plain edge inward (fig. 7). Pin and baste a length of pink ribbon over the edge of the lace at each corner. Topstitch or zig-zag stitch along both edges of ribbon, catching in edges of fabric and lace (fig. 8).

☐ Place trimmed square and plain back square together, right sides facing. Pin, baste and stitch all around, taking ⅝in seams and leaving an opening about 10in long in one side. Trim seam allowances and cut across each corner. Turn cover right side out.

☐ Insert pillow form. Turn in remaining raw edges; slipstitch together.

Pillow with lace motif trim

Finished size
15in square

Materials
½yd of 36in-wide pink fabric
16in square white lacy napkin
1¾yd of ¾in-wide eyelet insertion lace
1¾yd of ¼in-wide velvet ribbon
2¼yd of ⅜in-wide white lace edging
Lace remnants from which to cut motifs
15in-square pillow form
Matching thread

□From pink fabric cut out two pieces, each 16in square. Pin and baste the lacy napkin to the right side of one square (the front) (fig. 1).

□Thread the velvet ribbon through the eyelets in the insertion lace (fig. 2).

□Pin and baste the eyelet insertion lace right side up, all around the pillow front, 1in from the outer edge, mitering each corner. Stitch along edges (fig. 3).

□Cut out four large motifs and one small one from the remnant of lace. Place them in the center of the pillow front (fig. 4); pin, baste and hand-stitch in place.

□Pin the lace edging around the four sides of the square, ⅜in from the edge, placing right sides together, so that the finished edge of lace faces inward. Baste in place (fig. 5).

□Place trimmed front piece and back piece together with right sides facing and raw edges even. Pin, baste and stitch all around, taking a ⅝in seam and leaving an opening about 10in long in one side (fig. 6). Trim seam allowances and cut diagonally across each corner. Turn the pillow cover right side out.

□Insert pillow form. Turn in remaining raw edges and slipstitch them together.

Pillow with square trim

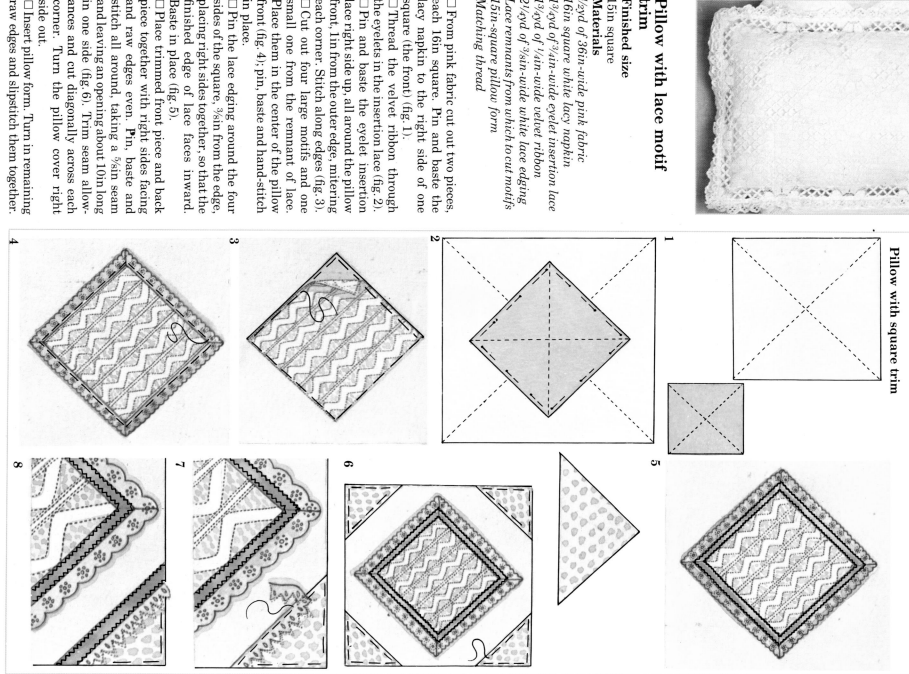

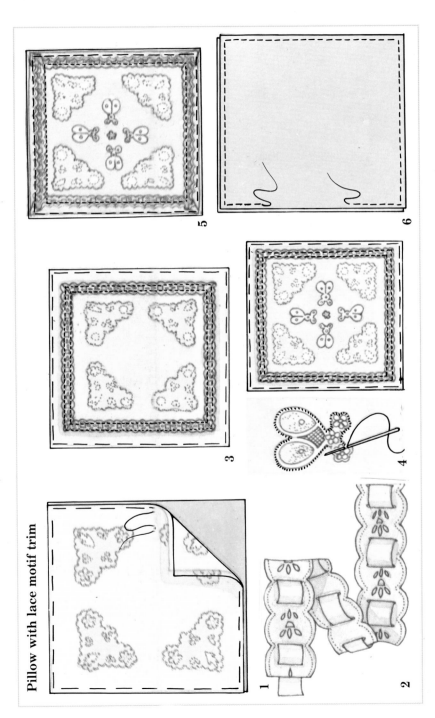

Pillow with lace motif trim

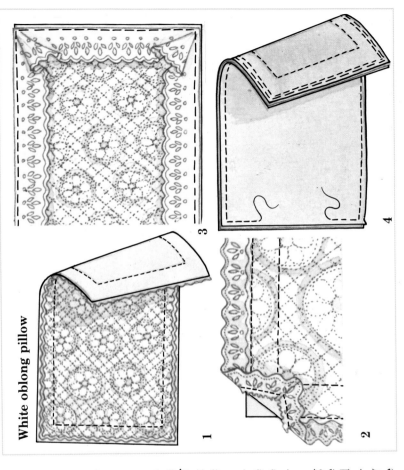

White oblong pillow

Finished size
18 × 14in, excluding lace edging

Materials
18½ × 14½in lace place mat
½yd of 36in-wide white fabric
2¼yd of 1in-wide gathered eyelet edging
2¼ of 1¾in-wide eyelet edging
18 × 14in pillow form.
Matching thread

☐ From white fabric cut out two rectangles, each 19 × 15in. Pin and baste the place mat, right side up, to right side of one rectangle (the front). Topstitch in place, 1in from the edge of the fabric (fig. 1).

☐ Pin, baste and stitch the gathered eyelet edging, right side upward, under the edge of the place mat, keeping it free from the cushion front fabric and mitering the corners (fig.2).

☐ Pin the 1¾in-wide eyelet edging around the pillow front, ⅜in from the edge, with right sides together and with finished edge of lace facing inward. Baste in place, being especially careful not to catch in the edge of the place mat as you do so (fig. 3).

☐ Place the front and back rectangles together with right sides facing. Pin, baste and stitch all around, taking a ½in seam and leaving an opening about 10½in long in one short side. While basting, take care to push all the lace edges toward the center so that they will not get caught in the stitching (fig. 4). Trim seam allowances and cut diagonally across each corner. Now turn the pillow cover so that it is facing right side out.

☐ Insert pillow form. Turn in the remaining raw edges and slipstitch them together.

Chapter 3

Bed and bath linen

Continental quilt

Coordinated bed linen

Patchwork quilt cover

Fitted bedspread

Fabric and crochet bedspread

Patchwork bedspread

Fitted double bedspread

Patchwork bedhead

Baby's coverlet

Quilted bassinet set

Jack and the beanstalk quilt

Animal sleeping bags

Monogrammed towels and pillowcases

Appliqué towels

Rainbow bath mat

Crochet bath mat

Continental Quilt

You can have the very latest in bedroom style ideas – and at a fraction of the cost – by making your own luxuriously warm Continental quilt. Making the quilt itself is almost as easy as making your bed is going to be!

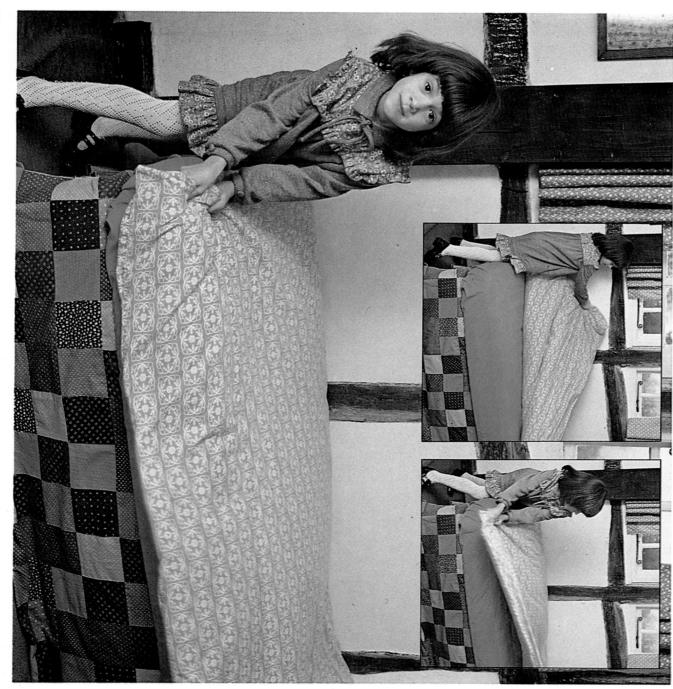

Finished size
About 54 × 84in, suitable for a standard twin bed

Materials
5yd of 54in-wide downproof cambric
2½lb of down and feather mixture
9¾yd of 2in-wide white cotton tape, cut into 4 × 84in lengths
Matching thread
Tailor's chalk
Note To make a double-size quilt, measuring 78 × 84in, you will need: 9¾yd of 48in-wide downproof cambric; 4lb of down and feather mixture; 17yd of 2in-

wide white cotton tape; thread.

☐ For twin quilt: on the wrong side of the fabric, mark off ¾in seam allowance down each long side. At one end, make four marks across the fabric width, at 10½in intervals. Repeat halfway down the fabric and at the opposite end. Join the marks to form four parallel lines running the length of the fabric (fig. 1).

☐ For double quilt: cut one length of fabric, 172in long. From the remaining fabric cut a piece 172in long by 27½in wide. Sew second length to first, down length, with a flat seam. Follow the directions given below for making the quilt, adjusting the number and widths of channels.

☐ Fold the fabric in half widthwise, right sides together. Stitch down one side with two rows of stitching, worked closely together, ½in from edges. This double row of stitching will prevent the filling from escaping (fig. 2).

☐ Turn the bag right side out. Place the bag with the opening toward you and join the two layers to make channels as described below, working from the stitched edge toward the open edge. At the first line on the bottom layer, pick up a small fold of fabric on the wrong side (inside). Take a piece of tape and pin one long edge of the tape behind this fold. Continue pinning the tape to the fabric in the same way along the first line to the bottom of the quilt. Stitch along the length, ¼in in from the tape edge close to the folded edge of fabric, forming a narrow pleat (fig. 3).

☐ Make a similar fold on the marked line of the upper layer. Pin the free edge of the tape behind this fold. Stitch in place, stitching as far into the fold at the bottom as possible. The first channel is now completed (fig. 4).

☐ Continue in this way across the fabric width, joining each pair of marked lines with a length of tape until the

first four channels have been formed. The reason for joining the layers with tape, instead of stitching them together, is to prevent cold areas along the seams (fig. 5).

☐ Turn in ½in along the two remaining outside edges and stitch together with two rows of stitching (fig. 6).

☐ Using clothespins, attach the quilt with the openings upward, to a clothesline or rope, first fixing the line at an accessible height. Working from one side to the other, push a handful of stuffing into the first channel, shake it down and clip the opening closed. Repeat this for the next channel and so on across the quilt. Return to the first channel and insert another handful. Continue until you have filled each channel evenly with the stuffing.

☐ Remove the quilt from the line. Turn under ½in along the upper edges and join the folded edges with two rows of stitching, worked close together.

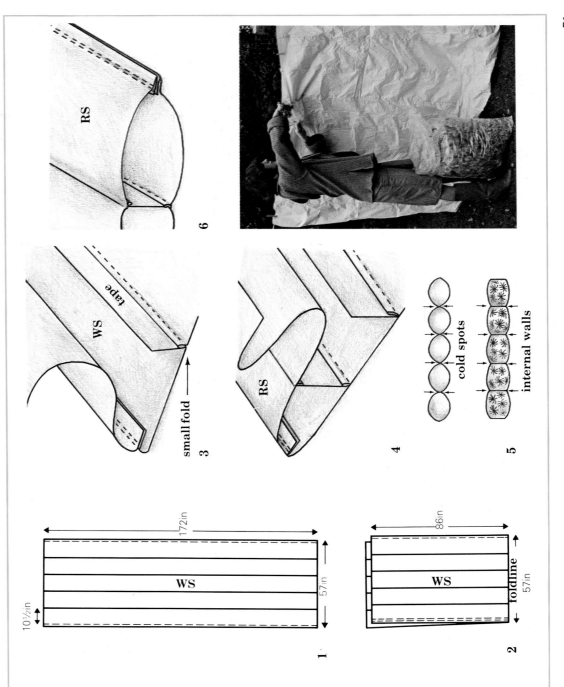

Coordinated Bed Linen

Make your bedroom up to the minute in fashion terms: create your own Continental quilt cover, with stylish coordinated bottom sheet and matching pillowcases.

Quilt Cover

Finished size
To fit a quilt 84in long, 54in wide

Materials
3½yd of 90in-wide printed suitable cotton polyester fabric
Remnants of solid color fabric to cover piping cord
8¼yd of narrow piping cord
1yd of ³⁄₄in-wide white gripper tape
Matching sewing thread

☐ From printed sheeting fabric cut out two pieces, each 88in long by 56in wide.
☐ From plain sheeting fabric cut 1½in-wide bias strips. Join them together on the straight grain to make a 8¼yd length.

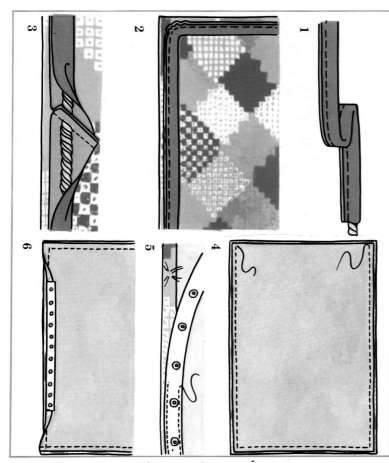

1
2
3
4
5
6

☐ Fold piping fabric with wrong side inside around piping cord, with long edges even. Pin and baste down complete length, close to cord (fig. 1).
☐ Pin and baste the covered piping cord around the edge on the right side of one printed fabric piece, with the cord lying inward and the basting line ³⁄₄in from outer edge (fig. 2).
☐ Where the covered piping cord meets, cut the cord to fit. Trim the fabric leaving small seam allowances; stitch the fabric leaving small seam allowances. Press seam flat. Hand-stitch cord ends together securely. Stitch piping in place around printed fabric piece.
☐ Place second printed fabric piece to first piped fabric piece with right sides together and outer edges even. Pin,

baste and stitch across top and down both long sides on existing stitching line, leaving remaining short side open (fig. 4).
☐ Turn under the seam allowance on remaining short side and press. Mark center point on one side.
☐ Separate the gripper tape and mark the center point of one side of tape. Matching centers, place this piece of tape to marked edge of open side. Position on the wrong side, covering the raw edges of the seam allowance. Tuck under raw ends of tape. Pin, baste and stitch the tape in place along all edges, close to the tape edge (fig. 5).
☐ Stitch the opposite side of tape in place on opposite side of cover, so the snaps will match.
☐ Pin, baste and stitch the remaining cover seam at either side of the tape (fig. 6).
☐ Finish all remaining raw edges of cover by zig-zag stitching them together.

Pillowcases

Finished size
30in long and 19in wide.

Materials
1½yd of 90in-wide solid color red fabric
Piece of printed fabric
24 × 12in
Matching sewing thread
Note This particular method of making pillowcases incorporates what is known as a 'housewife's flap'. This is a small flap which closes over the edge of the pillow and prevents it slipping out.

☐ For each pillowcase cut one piece of red sheeting fabric 72 × 20in.
☐ For each print corner motif cut a triangle of printed sheeting fabric measuring 10in long on each of the straight sides. Cut the long edge of both triangles into steps, if applicable, following the print fabric pattern; otherwise keep the long edge straight.
☐ To make each pillowcase, first fold under 3in along one short edge and turn under a ½in hem. Pin, baste and stitch hem in place across fabric (fig. 7).
☐ On the opposite short edge, fold under 7in. Pin and baste across folded edge. Turn a double ½in-wide hem on raw short edge. Pin, baste and stitch hem, but do not stitch the flap down to the main fabric (fig. 8).
☐ Fold the fabric in half widthwise, wrong sides together, with the folded edges even. Press fold. The pillowcase now measures 30½ × 20in allowing for

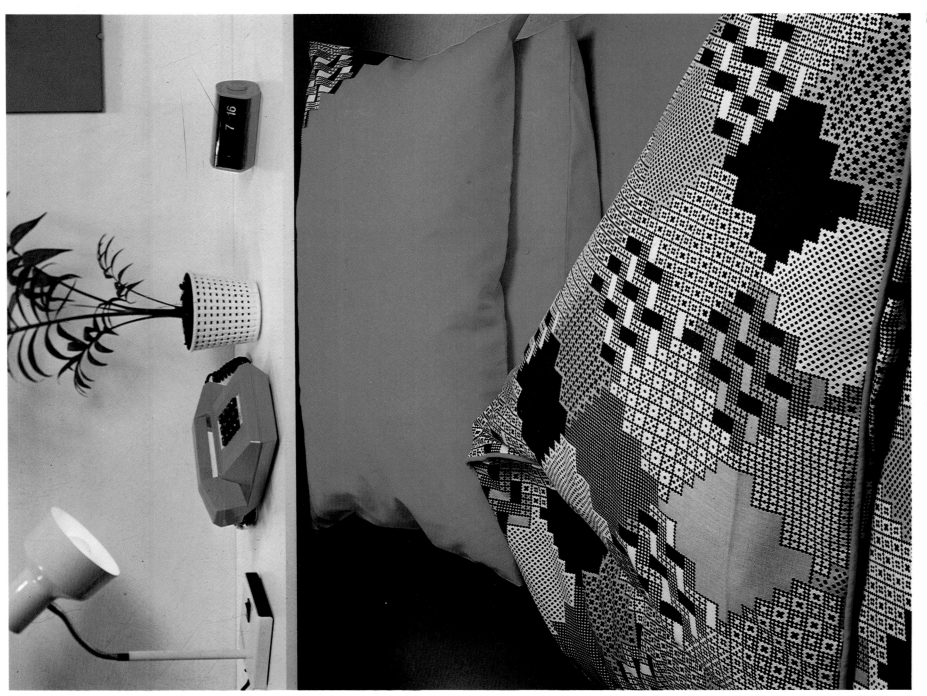

½in seam allowance on three sides.

□Open out the fabric, leaving the pressed crease in the center. Pin and baste the short edges of the contrasting triangle of fabric to the right side of the pillowcase, positioning the triangle in the top corner opposite the opening, with plain edges to top long edge and pressed folded edge (fig. 9).

□Turn under a narrow edge along the diagonal (stepped) edge. Pin, baste and stitch the diagonal edge to main fabric.

□Fold the pillowcase in half widthwise, with wrong sides together and the loose flap folded to wrong side. Pin, baste and stitch down long sides, ¼in from edges. Trim seams. Remove basting along fold (fig. 10).

□Turn pillowcase wrong side out, so the right sides are together. Fold the loose flap over, so that it covers the open short edge of the pillowcase. Pin, baste and stitch down the two long sides ¼in from the edge and across the folded edge ½in from the edge. This forms French seams and at the same time encloses the raw edges of the print triangle (fig. 11).

Fitted sheet

Finished size
To fit 3ft-wide bed

Materials
3yd of 90in-wide solid color red fabric
1yd of ⅜in-wide elastic
Matching sewing thread

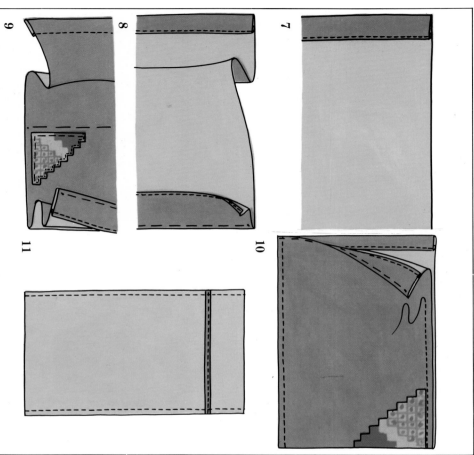

□Measure the length, width and depth of your mattress.

□To allow for a 6in tuck-in all the way around, cut a piece of fabric to the following size: the mattress length (6ft 6in) plus twice the mattress depth (6in) plus twice the tuck-in (6in)) by the mattress width (3ft) plus twice the depth (6in) plus twice the tuck-in (6in).

□Add the mattress depth (6in) and tuck-in allowance (6in) together and measure the resulting distance (12in) on each side of the corner points and mark. Measure the same distance (12in) in at a right angle from these two points so they meet, and mark again (fig. 12).

□At one corner, with right sides together, match the marked points on the outside edges together. Pin, baste and stitch the dart formed between the outer edge and the inside marked point (fig. 13).

□Cut up fold of dart. Fold in raw edges. Pin, baste and stitch together to finish. Repeat at each corner.

□To finish the outer edge of the sheet and form a channel for the elastic, turn a double ½in hem to the wrong side. Pin, baste and stitch all around the outer edge, close to edge.

□Measure 8in along each side from one corner point. Open up the stitched hem at these two points (fig. 14).

□Cut a 8in length of elastic for each corner. Pin one end of elastic to one opened point. Thread the elastic through the hem from this point around the corner to the second opening. Pin, baste and stitch the elastic securely in place at each end, across the hem (fig. 15). Repeat at each corner.

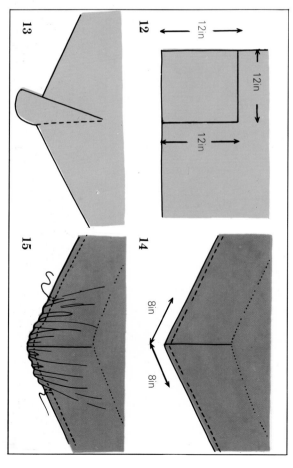

Patchwork Quilt Cover

This easy-to-make cover for a Continental quilt is a lovely way to introduce a touch of individuality into your bedroom. For the patches, you can use up remnants or have fun choosing a selection of new fabrics.

Finished size
78 × 78in, suitable for a double-bed quilt

Materials
2½yd of 90in-wide sheeting
49 squares of fabric, each 11in square
60 triangles of fabric, with shorter edges measuring 9in and the long edge measuring 13in
2¼yd straight tape
2½yd of 1in-wide bias binding
Matching sewing thread

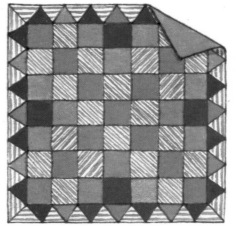

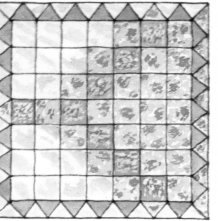

□ Start by planning the patchwork. Draw the pattern of squares and triangles shown (fig. 1) on a piece of paper. Use this to plan which patches are to be in each of your available fabrics, to get the best combination of colors and patterns. You can work out at this stage whether you have enough fabric or how much you need to buy.

Three alternative ideas for the patchwork scheme, showing different combinations of plain and patterned fabrics.

Once you have bought or selected the fabrics, wash them before cutting out, to avoid the risk of uneven shrinkage later.

□ Cut out your squares and triangles. When cutting the triangles, make sure one edge of each triangle is along the straight grain of the fabric. Make a paper pattern for the triangle to help you cut out accurately (fig. 2).

□ Finish the edges of each square and triangle by zig-zag stitching by machine or simply overcasting by hand (fig. 3).

□ Assemble the squares into the pattern required. With right sides together, sew the squares into seven strips, taking ⅝in seam allowance. Press seams open (fig. 4).

□ Matching seam lines, with right sides together, stitch the seven strips together. When this is done, press seams open (fig. 5).

□ With right sides together stitch the triangles together, overlapping corners as shown. Sew 15 triangles in each of four strips. Press (fig. 6).

□ With right sides together join the four strips at each corner to form a square. Press (fig. 7).

□ Stitch the outer square to the center squared sections, right sides together, matching seam lines. Trim and overcast the edges. Press the seams open (fig. 8).

□ Enclose one of the sides of the patchwork with bias binding – this is now the bottom edge (fig. 9).

□ Cut sheeting to measure 80 × 90in. Finish the edges by machine zig-zag or hand overcasting (fig. 10).

□ At one selvage, fold up ¾in and baste or pin, then fold up another ¾in and stitch to form a double hem. This is now the bottom edge of the sheeting (fig. 11).

□ Place patchwork and sheeting together with right sides facing and edges even at the top. Fold bottom 8in of sheeting over wrong side of patchwork to form flap. Baste and stitch down sides and along top (fig. 12).

□ Turn right side out and press. You can outline the patchwork with zig-zag or satin stitch on the right side if you wish (fig. 13).

□ Cut the tape into eight equal lengths. Sew four lengths at regular intervals 1in inside the flap edge, and four at matching intervals inside the patchwork edge. These tapes tie together to hold the quilt securely inside (fig. 14).

Note All fabrics should be colorfast, washable, and of the same weight. To make version as in photograph, buy 1⅝yd of patterned fabric for center patch; 1¼yd each of two other patterns and 1⅛yd of solid color fabric.

1

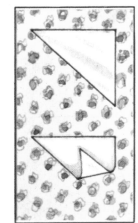

2

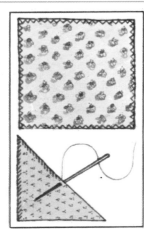

3

4

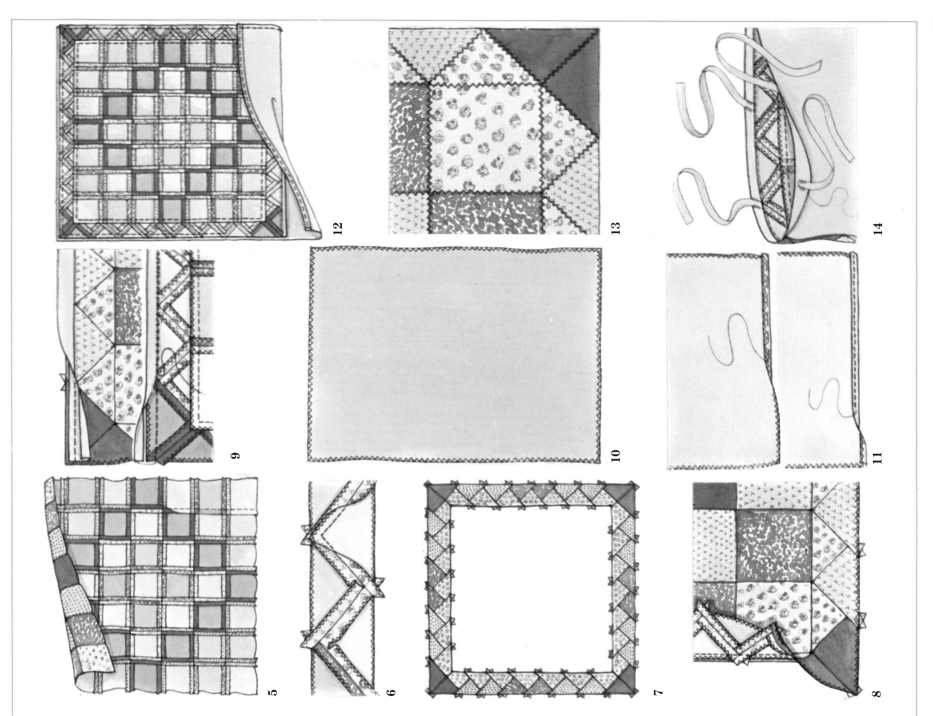

12

13

14

9

10

11

5

6

7

8

Fitted Twin Bedspread

Ideal for a study or guest room, this twin bedspread with piped edges and box pleats turns a spare bed into attractive seating.

Finished size

To fit a 75 × 36in studio bed. Height to top of mattress 21in. ¾in seam allowance is included.

Materials

9yd of 48in-wide printed furnishing cotton

13yd of piping cord

Matching sewing thread

□ For top: cut out one piece of fabric 76½ × 37½in. For sides: cut out two pieces each 76½ × 9½in and two pieces each 37½ × 9½in. For skirt: cut out eight pieces each 48 × 15½in.

□ From the remaining fabric cut out 2in-wide strips on the bias of the fabric for piping. Pin, baste and stitch the strips with right sides together to make about 6½yd length (fig. 1).

□ Fold the piping fabric in half around the piping cord, wrong side inside and edges even. Pin, baste and stitch down the complete length close to piping cord to hold it firmly in place.

□ Pin the covered piping around the sides, top and base of the top piece. Position the piping cord, starting at one corner with the piping lying inward (fig. 2).

□ Curve the piping slightly around each corner, snipping into the piping fabric seam allowance at each corner to help it curve around easily. Cut off excess piping cord; pin, baste and stitch the ends together to fit. Baste and stitch in place (fig. 3).

□ Place one long side piece to one short side piece with right sides together and matching one short edge. Pin, baste and stitch short edge (fig. 4). Repeat this whole procedure with remaining two side pieces.

□ Position the two combined side pieces with right sides together so that the short pieces are between the long pieces. Pin, baste and stitch the two remaining seams (fig. 5).

□ Place side piece to top piece over piped outer edge, with right sides to-

1

2

3

4

gether, positioning seams at the corners and with edges matching. Pin, baste and stitch in place (fig. 6).

□Pin length of covered piping around the remaining raw edge of side piece. Position the piping, starting at one corner with the piping facing inward and raw edges even. Pin, baste and stitch piping together to fit the edge. Baste and stitch the piping in place.

□Place two skirt pieces with right sides together, matching edges. Pin, baste and stitch together down one short edge (fig. 7). Repeat, stitching all skirt pieces together into one continuous ring.

□Turn under ⅜in on one long edge of skirt. Pin, baste and stitch in place (fig. 8). Turn up finished long edge of skirt 1in for hem. Pin, baste and hem in place by hand (fig. 9).

□Pin and baste box pleats along the length of the skirt. Begin at one seam and form fifteen box pleats for one side. Make each top pleat 5in wide and the underneath pleats 2in wide. Press pleats in position (fig. 10).

□For top end, continue around the skirt making seven box pleats with the top pleats 5⅛in wide and the underneath pleats 1¾in wide. Press pleats in position (fig. 11). Continue to complete the pleating around the skirt.

□Place the skirt to the piped edge of side piece with sides, top and base edges even. Position with right sides together, matching edges and easing pleats in position to fit, where necessary. Pin, baste and stitch skirt in place (fig. 12).

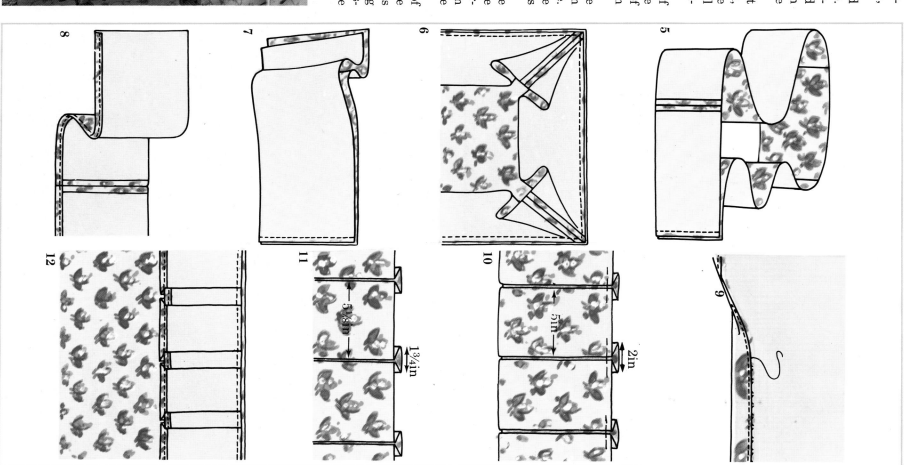

Fabric and Crochet Bedspread

Whether you buy fabric specially to match your bedroom or want to use up spare scraps or remnants, you'll see that fabric and crochet combine to make a bedspread to treasure.

Finished size
About 84in wide by 98in long
Materials
3050yd of a medium weight crochet cotton
42 pieces of fabric with hemmed edges, each 22in square
Size E crochet hook
Large-eyed tapestry needle

□ Thread needle with crochet cotton. Work blanket stitch around all four edges of each square, working 48 sts along each side and 3 sts at each corner.

Crochet
□ Join yarn to first st at one corner and using the crochet hook work 1ch to count as first sc, *2sc into last loop at

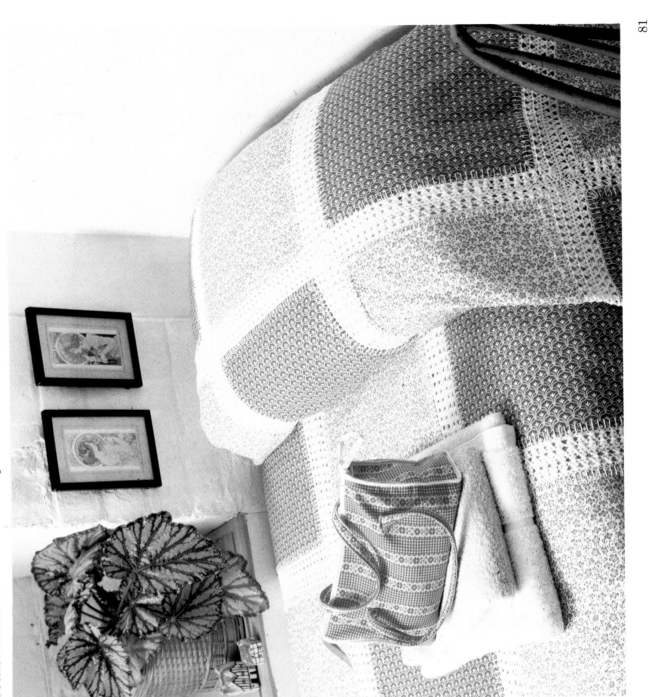

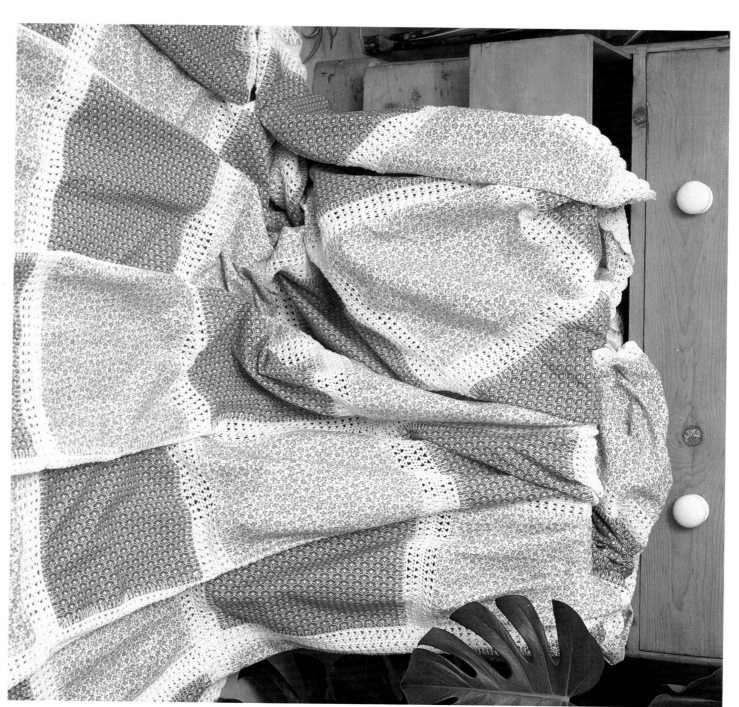

corner, ch 1, 2sc into first loop on next side, 1sc into each loop of next side, rep from * all around, sl st into first ch.

Next round Ch 2 to count as first dc, keeping hook at front of work, work 1dc into st before sl st – 2dc crossed –, skip next st, 1dc into next st, keeping hook at front of work, work 1dc into st that was skipped – 2dc crossed –, now work 2dc, ch 1 and 2dc all into corner sp, *(work 2 crossed dc) to next corner st, 2dc, ch 1 and 2dc all into corner sp, rep from * twice more, (work 2 crossed dc) to end, sl st into top of 3ch.

Next round As last round, working 2dc, ch 1 and 2dc into sp at corners. Fasten off. Edge all squares in the same way.

Making the bedspread

□ Arrange squares in pattern of your choice – we have alternated dark- and light-colored squares –, then join squares together in order to form a rect-angle 6 squares wide by 7 squares long.

Border

□ With RS of work facing, join yarn to first 2 crossed dc on one side, 1sc into same place as join, (skip next dc, 5dc into next dc, miss next dc, 1sc into next dc) to corner, work *7dc into corner sp (skip next dc, 5dc into next dc, skip next dc, sc into next dc) to corner, rep from * twice more, 7dc into corner sp, sl st into first sc.

□ Fasten off yarn; press fabric.

Patchwork Bedspread

This lovely patchwork bedspread is made in six toning fabrics using triangles, rectangles and squares. It is easy to machine stitch for quick – and beautiful – results.

Finished size
About 98 × 86in, to fit a double bed

Materials
2¾yd of 45in-wide fabric (A)
2¼yd of 45in-wide fabric (B)
1⅛yd of 45in-wide fabric (C)
1⅛yd of 45in-wide fabric (D)
3½yd of 45in-wide fabric (E)
⅝yd of 45in-wide fabric (F)
3yd of 90in-wide plain fabric for backing
Matching sewing thread
Thin cardboard; soft pencil
Ruler and tailor's square

□ Using a tailor's square and a ruler and thin cardboard, draw the patchwork patterns following the measurements given (fig. 1). Carefully cut out each pattern.

□ Using a soft pencil and working on the wrong side of the fabric, draw around each pattern on the appropriate fabric to give the correct number of patches (see below). When marking, place the patterns on the straight grain of the fabric and leave a ⅜in margin all around each one.

□ From fabric A cut out 16 large plain squares. Cut out 144 triangles.

□ From fabric B cut out 12 large plain squares. Cut out 108 triangles.

□ From fabric C cut out 144 triangles.

□ From fabric D cut out 108 triangles.

□ From fabric E cut out 127 border rectangles.

□ From fabric F (which should be plain) cut out 72 border squares.

□ Using two different triangles together, one fabric A and one fabric C, join them together to form a square. Place the two triangles with right sides together, matching all edges. Pin, baste and stitch down the diagonal edge (fig. 2).

□ Repeat to make all the triangles in fabric A and C into squares.

□ Make more squares in the same way using triangles in fabrics B and D.

□ Join three triangle squares in fabrics A and C together into a strip. Place two squares with right sides together, edges matching and with the diagonal seams running from top right to bottom left. Pin, baste and stitch together. Repeat to stitch third square to the previous two (fig. 3). Form two more strips in fabrics A and C.

□ Join these three strips together to form one large square. Place two strips with right sides together, long edges matching. Make sure that the horizontal seams match together, and the diagonal seams are all running in the same direction – from top right to bottom left. Pin, baste and stitch along edges. Repeat to stitch third strip to previous two strips (fig. 4).

□ Make another 15 large triangle patchwork squares in fabrics A and C.

□ Make 12 large squares in fabrics B and D.

□ Place one border rectangle to top edge of one large rectangle patchwork square. Position with right sides together, edges matching. Pin, baste and stitch together.

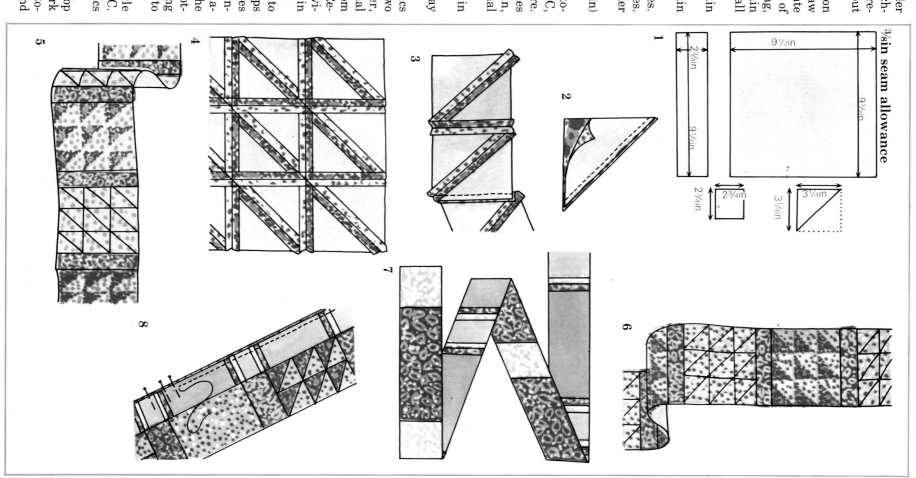

⅜in seam allowance

9½in

9½in

2¾in 2¾in

2¾in 2¾in

9½in

3¼in

3¼in

1

2

3

4

5

6

7

8

☐ Repeat to join a border rectangle to the top edge of each large triangle patch square in the same way.

☐ Repeat to join one border rectangle to one side of each plain large square in the same way.

☐ Join four triangle patch squares in fabrics A and C with border rectangles to four plain large squares in fabric A with border rectangles, alternating the large squares and positioning them so that the border rectangles are always between the squares (fig. 5). Begin the strip with a plain large square. Place the first two squares/rectangles with right sides together and edges matching. Pin, baste and stitch together. Repeat until there are eight squares in each strip. Pin, baste and stitch a border rectangle to the base edge of the final square.

☐ Make a similar strip using triangle patch squares in fabric B and D and plain squares in fabric B, but begin the strip with a triangle patch square (fig. 6). Make five more strips in the same way.

☐ Join eight border rectangles to nine border squares to form a strip, alter-

nating the two shapes and with a border square at each end. Place the first square to the first rectangle with right sides together and edges matching. Pin, baste and stitch together. Repeat to complete the strip (fig. 7). Make seven more strips in the same way.

☐ With right sides facing, join right-hand long edge of one strip of border rectangles and squares to left-hand long edge of patches and border rectangles strip in fabrics A and C, so there is a plain square at the top. Place with right sides together and edges matching. Pin, baste and stitch together (fig. 8).

☐ Make six more double strips in the same way, stitching the rectangles and squares strip to the right-hand side of each strip of squares. Make sure that when stitched together the plain squares will alternate with the patchwork squares horizontally across the bedspread.

☐ Join the resulting double strips together, alternating the fabrics and plain squares with patchwork squares. Place the first two strips with right sides together, long edges matching

and with the border strips in between the two strips of squares. Pin, baste and stitch together. Repeat to complete the patchwork.

☐ Join the remaining border rectangles and squares strip to the left-hand edge of the finished patchwork. Place with right sides together and long edges even. Pin, baste and stitch together.

☐ Lay the backing fabric flat with wrong side up. Place the patchwork with right side up over the backing fabric. Pin and baste the two layers together.

☐ Measure 2½in from the last border seam and mark all around. Trim the backing fabric to within ¾in of the raw edge of the patchwork.

☐ Turn under the edge of the backing fabric for ⅜in and fold over onto the patchwork to marked edge, mitering the corners neatly. Pin, baste and stitch the hem in place using a zig-zag machine stitch.

A patchwork bedspread will look particularly beautiful in color-coordinated fabrics of a similar design.

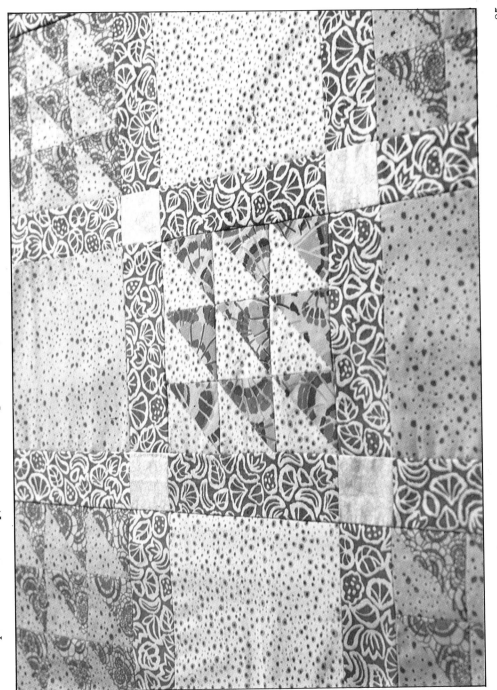

Fitted Double Bedspread

Give your bedroom a stylish tailored look with a fitted bedspread. This bedspread is lined throughout and has a pillow flap which folds down to cover the pillows. The corners are finished in a plain, matching fabric, and piping from the same fabric is applied around the top.

Materials

For a standard double bed, using a fabric with a 25in pattern repeat:

15½yd of 48in-wide main fabric
12yd of 48in-wide lining fabric
2¼yd × 48in-wide plain fabric for the corners and piping
6yd piping cord
Matching sewing thread

Patterned chintz or a floral cotton will add interest to a plain room, but choose a solid color cotton, linen or sateen to enhance patterned bedroom furnishings. Bold designs can look very effective, but a small pattern is more economical and less difficult to match for the beginner.

The matching fabric should be of the same weight as the main fabric. To suit the size of the bed, it is advisable to buy fabric which is 48in wide or wider. The lining fabric must be the same width, and 48in is the width most readily available.

For the lining, choose a cotton sateen curtain lining in white, cream or a matching color. Do not choose synthetic lining fabric which would be very slippery on the bed.

Measuring the bed

☐ With the bedclothes in place, measure the length and width of the bed, and the height from the top edge to the floor. Draw a sketch of how the bedspread will look when laid out flat (fig. 1). If the bed is wider than the fabric, follow the seamlines shown in the diagram when joining widths. The calculations below are for a standard double bed.

Estimating fabric

☐ All seam allowances throughout are ⅝in unless otherwise stated and all hems 2in. If a larger seam allowance seems suitable, allow for this when calculating fabric quantities. If you have chosen a fabric with a large design, allow extra pattern repeats for matching the pattern.

Top and bottom panel

☐ To make it easy to match the pattern, these two pieces are cut as one length, and then cut across where the top meets the bottom panel. Allow two widths of fabric which measure the length of the bed, plus the height, plus hem, plus 1¾in for seam allowances.

Side panels

☐ These will need two widths of fabric each, as the pattern falls vertically. Allow the height of the bed, plus hem, plus seam allowance for each panel.

Pillow flap

☐ Allowance must be made at each side to accommodate the height of the pillow (this is about 7in) and the flap should be the width of the bed plus twice the height of the bed, plus 14in (twice the allowance for pillow height), plus 4in for side hems, plus seam allowances: three widths of fabric, 30in long are required.

Corner pieces

☐ Allow one width of fabric for each corner piece, the height of the bed, plus the width, plus 4in.

Piping

To calculate how much piping cord you need, measure twice the length of the bed, plus the width, plus 4in.

Making the bedspread

☐ Cut a piece of the main fabric according to the measurements above. Matching the pattern, cut another piece the same length. With the right sides together, join both pairs of selvages, matching the pattern carefully. With the fabric in a tube shape, trim and press the seams open, then lay seams together and pin (fig. 2).

☐ Measure up from the bottom, which way the design is running), and mark a line the height of the bed plus a 2in hem, plus a ⅝in seam allowance. Cut across this line through both layers of fabric (fig. 3). Put aside the smaller piece for the bottom panel.

☐ Measure half the width of the bed, plus seam allowance from the fold across the fabric. Mark a line and cut through both layers of fabric (fig. 4).

side panel
bottom panel
top panel
pillow flap
side panel
1
2

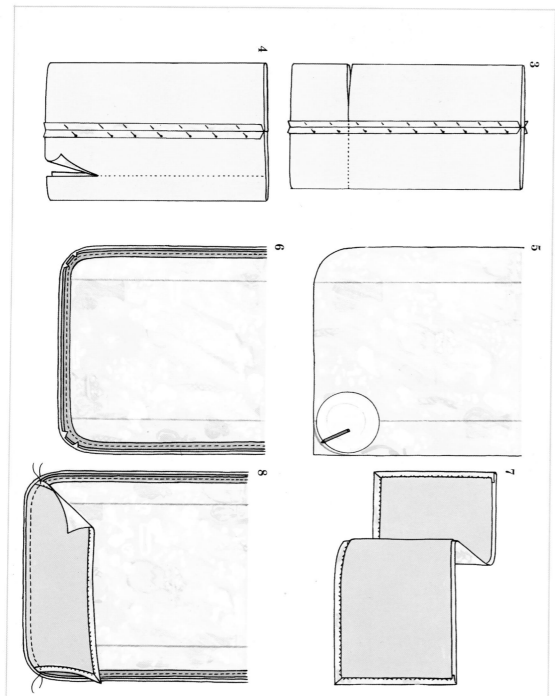

3 4 5 6 7 8

□ Unpin the seams. Using a plate and a pencil, draw a small curve around the bottom corners (fig. 5).

□ Make the required length of piping and stitch it to three sides of the top piece. Take care not to pull the piping, otherwise puckering will result. Clip the corners of the piping fabric (fig. 6).

□ Cut two widths of lining, each piece 2in shorter in length than the main fabric. With right sides together, join the selvages as for the main fabric. Press the seams open and pin.

□ Measure up from the bottom and mark a line the height of the bed, plus seam allowance. Cut across this line. Put aside the smaller piece for the bottom panel. Fold and cut the larger piece as for the main fabric.

□ Fold and pin the main fabric for the bottom panel in the same way as for the top panel. From the fold, measure half the width of the bed, plus 2in for side hems. Mark a line and cut. Unpin and open out. Press a 2in hem to the wrong side along the bottom and two sides, mitering the corners. Follow the same procedure for the lining, omitting side hems. Press ⅜in to the wrong side length of the bed, plus 2in for side hems. Cut along this line. Press a 2in hem to the wrong side along the bottom and two sides, mitering the corners.

□ Place the lining, right side up, on the wrong side of the main fabric so that ⅜in of the main fabric extends outside the lining along three sides. Slipstitch the lining to the main fabric and to close the miters (fig. 7).

□ Place the bottom panel on the top with right sides together and seamlines matching. Pin and baste the bottom panel in place. Using the zipper foot and following the seamline of the piping, machine stitch the two pieces together (fig. 8).

□ Make sure that the pattern is the same on both side panels. For each panel, cut two widths of main fabric. Place right sides together and join the selvages as before. Press the seams open. Fold and pin in the same way as for the bottom panel. From the fold, measure and mark a line half the length of the bed, plus seam allowance. Cut across this line. Join the lining and the main fabric in the same way as for the bottom panel.

□ Cut two widths of lining, the same height as the bed, plus seam allowance. Join the selvages. Press the seams open, fold in the same way as the main fabric and pin. Measure and mark a line half the length of the bed; cut. Open out the lining. Press ⅜in to the wrong side along the bottom and sides.

□ Join the lining and the main fabric in the same way as for the bottom panel.

□ Starting at one corner where the bottom panel ends, and with right sides together, pin, baste and machine stitch one side panel to the top. Use the zipper foot and follow the seamline of the piping (fig. 9). Repeat on the other side of the bedspread.

□ Taking care to match the pattern, cut three widths of main fabric, 30in long. Join the pieces together down the two sets of selvages. Press the seams open. Matching the seams, fold the fabric in half and pin. From the fold, measure half the width of the bed, plus the height of the bed, plus a 7in allowance for the pillow height, plus 2in for side hems. Mark a line and cut. Unpin and open out the fabric. Press a 2in hem to the wrong side along the bottom and two sides, mitering the corners (fig. 10).

□ Cut three widths of lining, and join along the selvages in the same way as for the main fabric. Fold in half, matching the seamlines, and pin. From the fold, measure as before, omitting side hems. Unpin and open out the lining. Press a ⅜in hem along the bottom and two sides.

□ Join the lining and main fabric in the same way as bottom and side panels.

□ Place the pillow flap, right side up, on the right side of the top where the side panels end, matching the seams. Pin, baste and machine stitch the two pieces together. Snip both fabrics of the pillow flap at the top corners of the top piece, allowing the raw edges to be turned in. Slipstitch down the openings to close (fig. 11).

□ Using the plain, matching fabric, cut four squares the height of the bed, plus seam allowance all around. Place the pieces, right sides together, in pairs. Pin, baste and stitch around three sides of each piece. Trim the corners and turn the fabric so it is right side out. Press.

□ Mark the center point of one corner piece. Fold the side panel and bottom panel over to the right side of the top. Pin the corner piece in position with the center mark exactly at the point where the side and bottom panels meet. Stitch along the

piped seam. Repeat this procedure for the other corner (fig. 12).

□ Take the piece of lining set aside earlier. Fold in half, matching seamlines, and pin. From the center, measure half the width of the bed plus seam allowance. Mark a line and cut. Unpin and unfold the lining. Place it on the top, wrong sides together and seams matching. Pin the lining to the main fabric parallel to one seamline and fold it back. Using a strong thread, lockstitch the lining to the main fabric through the seam allowances. Repeat the process along the other seam (fig. 13).

Grade the seam allowances all around the top and press toward the center. Fold under the seam allowance of the lining all around, covering all raw edges. Pin and slipstitch all around the top to give a neat and professional appearance to the finished bedspread.

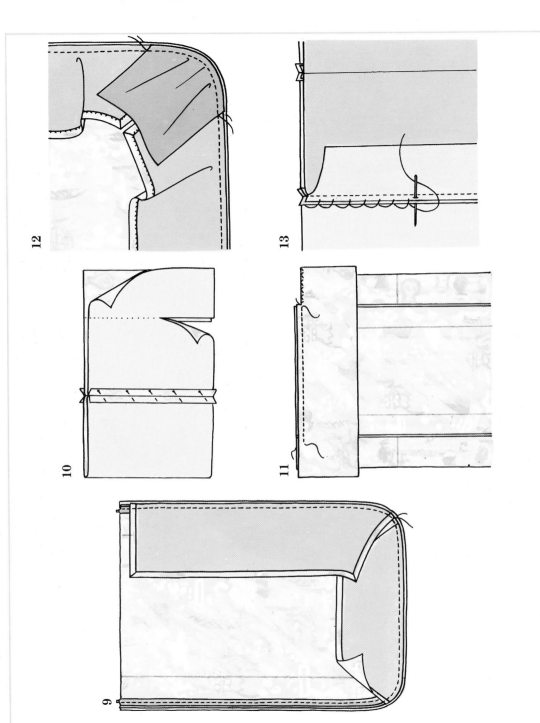

12

13

10

11

9

Patchwork Bedhead

This attractive bedhead is simply two pillows which have been hung from a decorative drapery rod. The pillows are worked in traditional log cabin patchwork design and this can be easily sewn by machine stitching.

Finished size
Each pillow is about 28 × 21in

Materials
2¾yd of 45in-wide solid color dark cotton poplin
¾yd of 45in-wide cotton print fabric in seven harmonizing prints: three dark and four light colored (5¼yd total)
⅜yd of 45in-wide solid color light cotton fabric
1¼yd of 45-in wide white cotton fabric for backing
Matching sewing thread
Two pieces of 3in-thick foam, each 28 × 21in

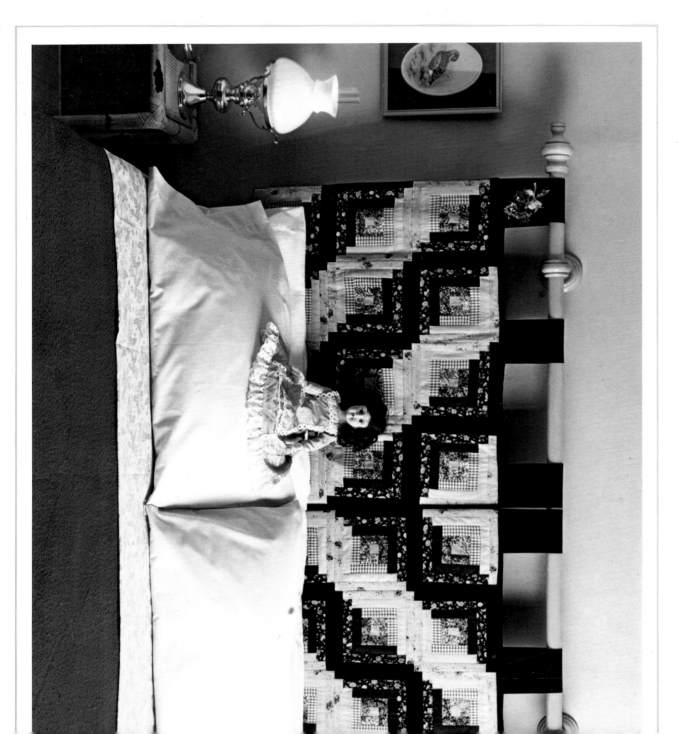

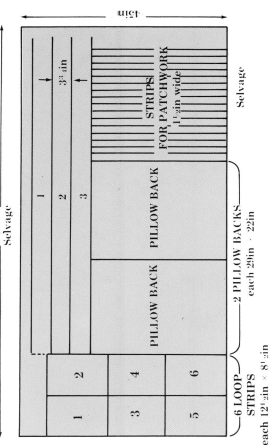

□ Cut out the pieces from solid color dark cotton poplin fabric, following the cutting layout.
□ Cut out 48 strips 1½in wide and 8in long from each of the print fabrics, cutting parallel to the grain of the fabric. From solid color light cotton fabric cut out 24 pieces 1½in square for the center. From white cotton backing fabric cut out 24 pieces 8½in square. Measure and draw the squares carefully and accurately on the fabric before cutting them out.
□ On one side of each white backing square, using a pencil, lightly draw two diagonal lines from corner to

establish the center point. Place one solid light square centrally on one marked backing square, matching center points and the straight grain; baste (fig. 1). The diagonals will also help to keep the design symmetrical.
□ Choose your arrangement of fabrics so that two adjoining sides are in light colors and the opposite adjoining sides are in a darker or contrasting color; this forms the basis of the design. You will end up with all the dark 'logs' in one half of the square and the light 'logs' in the opposite half.
□ Place the first strip face down on center square matching raw edges,

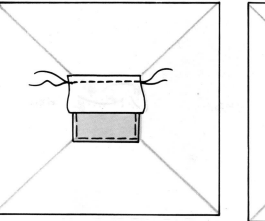

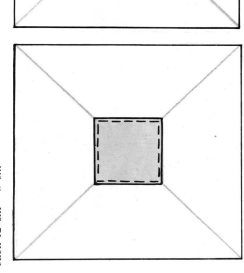

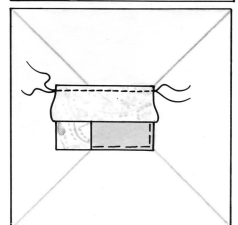

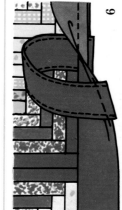

9

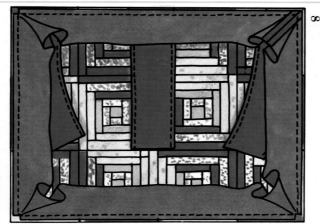

8

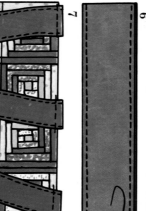

7

6

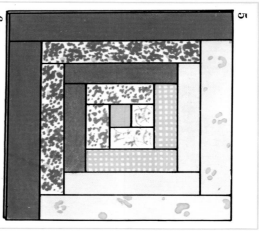

5

Alternative log cabin design ideas

trimming off excess strip to fit. Pin, baste and stitch along seamline (fig. 2). Fold strip over to right side.

□ Similarly, working in a clockwise direction, pin, baste and stitch second strip in the same fabric to the second side of the center square and the end of the first strip (fig. 3).

□ Continue around the square, working the next two strips in a darker or contrasting fabric, again trimming the strips to the correct length. This completes the first round (fig. 4).

□ Continue this pattern, working around the square in a clockwise direction, until you have used all the differ-

ent fabric strips. Always use light fabrics for the first two sides and the darker or contrasting fabrics for the opposite sides. The finished square will measure about 8in (fig. 5). It is important to keep the strips parallel to the sides of the original square in the center to ensure that the final shape is accurate, although you may find each patchwork square varies slightly. Make 23 more squares.

□ Arrange 12 of the patchwork squares in an interesting pattern. Place two adjoining squares with right sides together, matching edges; pin, baste and stitch them together. Repeat to stitch

Log cabin was a popular patchwork design in the United States in the second half of the nineteenth century. Strips of fabric are built out from a central square, their edges overlapping. The square is divided diagonally by the light and dark shading of the strips. The square represents the fire, the light half of the square is the firelit side of the room and the dark half the shadows.

all 12 patchwork squares together to form the front, measuring 29 × 22in. Repeat for second front.

☐ Fold one loop piece in half widthwise with right sides together. Pin, baste and stitch long edges. Turn loop strip right side out. Topstitch ½in from both long edges (fig. 6). Make five more loop strips in the same way.

☐ With right sides together, pin and baste one short edge of three loop strips along the top edge of the patchwork front, with the two outer loop strips ½in from side edges of pad front and the third loop strip halfway between the two (fig. 7).

☐ With right sides together, pin, baste and stitch gusset strip pieces together to form one long strip.

☐ With right sides together and leaving a ½in overlap at the first corner, pin, baste and stitch the gusset strip around the patchwork front. It is easier to work one side at a time, snipping the gusset seam allowance in toward the line of stitching at each corner point to give good sharp corners. At the end of the fourth side, cut away excess gusset strip, leaving ½in for seam. Use remaining strip for second pad.

☐ Pin, baste and stitch short edges of gusset strip together to fit pillow front.

Finish stitching gusset to front (fig. 8).
☐ Fold loop strips up to meet the other side of the gusset; pin and baste in place (fig. 9). With right sides together pin, baste and stitch pillow back to gusset, catching in loops and matching corners with corner positions on gusset. Leave a 27in opening along the bottom edge.

☐ Turn cover right side out. Insert foam. Fold in opening edges and slip-stitch together to close.
☐ Repeat for second pad.
☐ Fix the pole to the wall securely, at the correct height for a bedhead, and slip the pads over it.

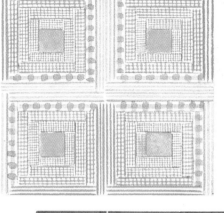

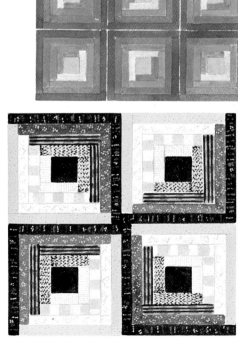

Baby's Coverlet

Our charming crib or carriage cover is made in bright mix-and-match cotton fabrics. The center piece of the cover is carefully worked patchwork in the cathedral window design. The result: a very pretty heirloom.

Finished size
About 27½in by 22in

Materials
1yd of 36in-wide white cotton lawn
⅝yd of 45in-wide red on white floral cotton print
⅝yd of 45in-wide blue on white floral cotton print
¾yd of 45in-wide blue floral cotton print
½yd of 45in-wide contrasting white and blue floral cotton print
3yd of ⅜in-wide red velvet ribbon
¾yd of 45in-wide medium-weight polyester batting

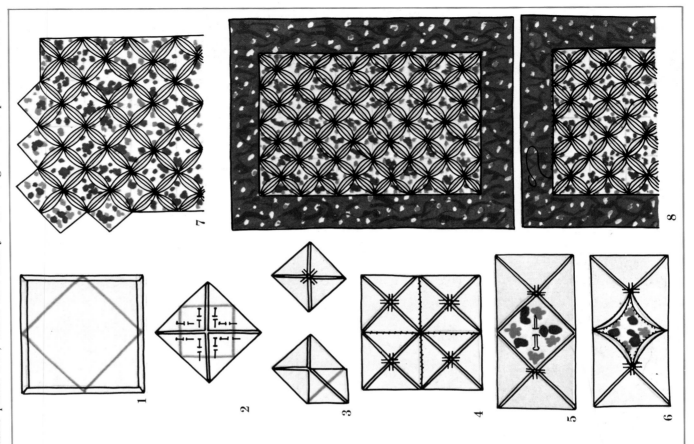

Matching sewing thread
Graph paper and thin cardboard for patterns

□ Make a square pattern. Draw and cut out a 6¼in square from graph paper. Using this as a guide, cut out your pattern from thin cardboard.

□ From white cotton lawn, using the pattern, cut out twenty-four squares. Align the sides of the pattern with the straight grain of the fabric.

□ Make a second pattern, 1¾in square.

□ Using the 1¾in pattern, cut out a selection of squares from the red on white and blue on white floral print cotton fabrics.

□ On one white square fold all the edges under ¼in (fig. 1). Fold in each corner of the square to meet in the center. Pin to hold. The square now measures 4⅛in (fig. 2).

□ Fold each corner of this square in toward the center. Pin to hold, removing the previous pins. Fasten the corners together at the center with a few neat stitches to hold them. The square now measures 3in. It is important to maintain accuracy at this stage to achieve a good result. Repeat to fold all the white squares in the same way.

□ Begin stitching the squares together: position four white squares together, matching sides. Stitch the squares together on their adjoining sides with small overcasting stitches (fig. 4). Repeat until the twenty-four squares have been joined together to form a rectangle six squares long and four squares wide.

□ Work out a pleasing pattern with the red on white and blue on white floral cotton print squares. Position the floral squares in the center of the stitched-together squares, over the overcasting stitches. Pin in place (fig.5). Move the floral squares around until a good design has been achieved. Baste the floral squares in position. At the side edges, only half of the floral squares will be attached.

□ Begin at one floral square: roll and turn an adjoining folded edge of the white fabric over the raw edge of the floral square. It will form a gentle curve. Taking small stitches, stitch the white fabric in position, right through all the fabric thicknesses. Work around all the four sides of the floral square (fig. 6).

□ Repeat with all floral squares of fabric. At the side edges, roll over the two sides only. Fold the remaining half of each square to the wrong side; pin and baste in place (fig.7).

□ When the patchwork is completed, press the work gently on the wrong side with a steam iron or over a damp cloth.

□ From blue floral print fabric cut out two pieces each 23 × 17½in for backing. Align the sides of each piece with the straight grain of the fabric.

□ Place one blue floral print fabric piece with right side on top. Position the wrong side of the patchwork fabric centrally on the right side of the blue fabric piece. Pin, baste and neatly stitch the patchwork fabric in place around all side edges (fig.8).

□ Cut the velvet ribbon into four lengths: two 28½in long and two 23in long.

□ Starting at one corner of patchwork center, leave about 5½in of ribbon free at each side, pin and baste one short length of ribbon along short edge of patchwork center over the previous stitches. Hand stitch both sides of the ribbon in place. Repeat at opposite short edge of patchwork fabric and – using the long lengths of ribbon – at each long side of the patchwork center.

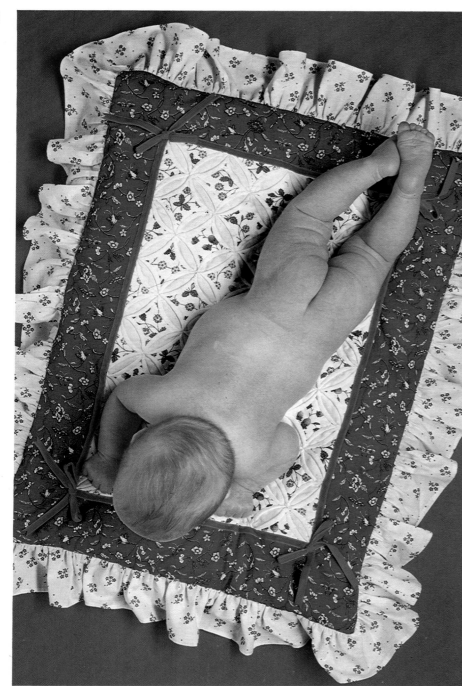

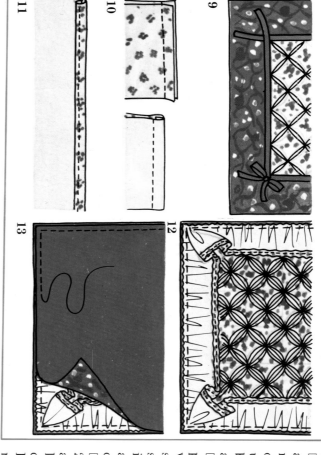

9

10

11

12

13

□ Tie the excess ribbon at each corner into a neat bow. Hand stitch the bows neatly in place (fig. 9).

□ For the ruffle, from the contrasting white and blue floral cotton print cut out four strips 3½in wide from across the width of the fabric.

□ Position two ruffle pieces with wrong sides together, matching edges. Pin, baste and stitch one short edge, taking ¼in seam allowance. Refold, with right sides together and stitch again, taking just over ¼in seam allowance to form a French seam (fig. 10).

□ Repeat to stitch all the ruffle pieces together in the same way, forming a ring shape.

□ Fold under a double ¼in hem along one edge of the ruffle piece: fold under the edge for ¼in, turn under again for ¼in. Pin, baste and topstitch hem (fig. 11).

□ Run two rows of gathering stitches along raw edge of ruffle piece. Place raw edge of ruffle with right side to outer edge of patchworked piece. Pull up gathering stitches evenly to fit. Pin, baste and stitch, taking ½in seam allowance (fig. 12).

□ Position second blue floral cotton print piece with right side to patch-work piece, over ruffle. Pin, baste and stitch all around following existing stitching line, leaving an 8in opening in one short side (fig. 13). Trim seam allowance and cut across corners. Turn quilt right side out.

□ From batting cut out two pieces each 22 × 16½in. Place pieces together with all edges even. Insert double batting layer into quilt, pushing well into the corners. Fold in the opening edges. Finally, slipstitch the folded edges neatly together.

Quilted Bassinet Set

Make a pretty bedding set from mix-and-match sheeting for baby's first crib – bumpers for extra protection and two quilts, a mattress cover and sheets to match

Finished size
To fit a crib 15in wide, 30in long and 10in deep, measured on the inside

Materials
1yd of 90in-wide floral sheeting
¾yd of 90in-wide small floral sheeting for set of bumpers
¾yd of 90in-wide solid color sheeting, for mattress cover
1½yd of 36in-wide medium-weight batting
1¾yd of ½in-wide bias binding
Matching sewing thread

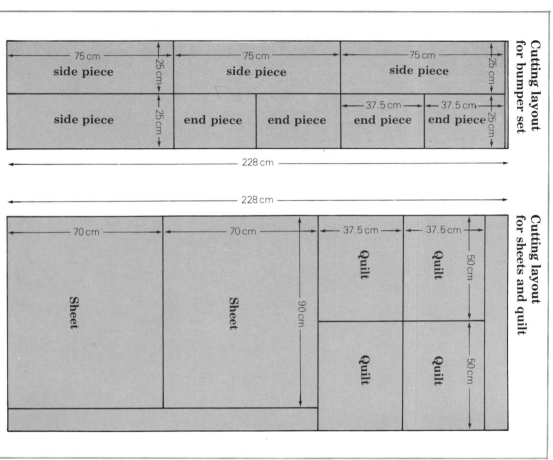

Cutting layout for bumper set

side piece — 75 cm — 25 cm
side piece — 75 cm — 25 cm
side piece — 75 cm — 25 cm
side piece
end piece — end piece
end piece — 37.5 cm — end piece — 37.5 cm — 25 cm
228 cm

Cutting layout for sheets and quilt

228 cm
Sheet — 70 cm
Sheet — 70 cm
Quilt — 37.5 cm — 50 cm
Quilt — 37.5 cm — 50 cm
Quilt
Quilt
90 cm

Bumper set

□Cut out side and end pieces for bumpers from small floral patterned sheeting, following the cutting layout.

□From batting cut out two pieces each 30 × 10in for side pieces and two pieces 15 × 10in for end pieces.

□Place batting side piece in between two fabric side pieces, matching outer edges and with right sides on the outside. Pin and baste together, taking large stitches (fig. 1).

□Sew lines of diagonal stitching across the side piece, through all the three thicknesses, spacing the lines of stitching 2in apart (fig. 2). Sew lines of diagonal stitching across the side piece, at a right angle to the first rows of stitching, to form a quilted diamond pattern (fig. 3).

□Repeat to make the second side piece and end pieces in the same way.

□For ties, cut out eight 12in lengths from bias binding. On one tie piece, fold in one short edge for ⅜in and baste. Fold the tie piece in half lengthwise, wrong side inside. Baste and stitch together down complete length (fig. 4). Make seven more ties in the same way.

□Position raw short edge of one tie in the center of each short side of each bumper piece. Pin and baste in place with the facing center of piece (fig. 5).

□Pin, baste and stitch one side of bias binding all around the outer edge of side piece, with right sides together and raw edges even, catching in ends of ties. Miter the corners and join the short edges of bias binding to fit (fig. 6).

□Fold binding over the outer edge; pin, baste and slipstitch to the stitch line on the opposite side. Bind the outer edge of second side piece and both end pieces in the same way.

□Position the bumpers inside the crib, tying the ties in each corner.

Sheet

□Cut out both sheet pieces from floral sheeting, following the cutting layout. These measurements include seam allowance.

□Fold under a double hem all around the edge of each sheet for ⅜in and then ¾in. Pin and baste in place, mitering the corners. Stitch in position.

Mattress cover

□For mattress cover cut out one piece 70 × 20in from solid color sheeting. On each short side of the mattress cover turn under a double hem, for ⅜in and then ¾in. Pin, baste and stitch both the hems in position (fig. 1).

□To form tuck-in, measure 30in in from one short side and pin to mark. Fold fabric at this mark, wrong sides together. Turn the 7¾in of excess fabric inside. Pin, baste and stitch down each long side, taking a ⅜in seam (fig. 2).

□Re-fold the mattress cover to the wrong side. Pin, baste and stitch down each long side again, this time taking ¾in seam allowance (fig. 3).

□Fold cover to right side. The tuck-in allows the mattress cover to be removed easily for washing.

Quilt

□Cut out quilt pieces from floral sheeting, following cutting layout. From batting cut out one piece 18 × 15in.

□Place batting piece between the two fabric pieces, matching all outer edges and with right sides on the outside. Pin and baste together (fig. 1).

□Sew lines of diagonal stitching across the fabric, through all thicknesses, spacing the lines of stitching 2in apart. Sew lines of diagonal stitching across the fabric, at a right angle to the first rows of stitching, to form a quilted diamond pattern (fig. 2).

□Pin and baste one side of the bias binding all around the outer edge of quilt, with right sides together and raw edges even. Miter the corners and join the short edges of bias binding together to fit. Stitch the first side of the bias binding in position.

□Fold the bias binding over the outer edge of the quilt; baste and slipstitch the remaining edge of the bias binding to the stitching line on the opposite side (fig. 3).

□Repeat for second quilt.

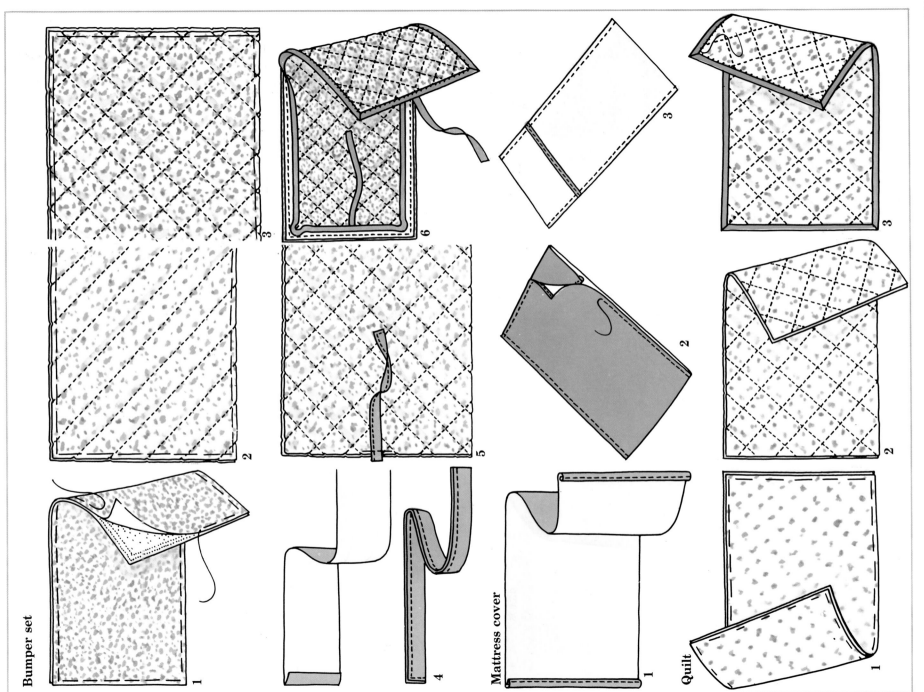

Bumper set

1

2

3

5

6

3

3

2

2

Mattress cover

1

Quilt

1

4

Jack and the Beanstalk Quilt

A child's delight! The colorful details of this quilt will bring "Jack and the Beanstalk" to life – and add a new dimension to bedtime reading.

Quilt

Finished size
65in long by 42in wide. Suitable for a twin bed.

Materials
3½yd of 45in-wide light blue heavyweight poplin
½yd of 45in-wide green heavyweight poplin
2yd of 45in-wide red heavyweight poplin
3¾yd of 60in-wide polyester batting
Scraps of other fabrics for appliqué (see directions for details)
One wooden bead
Scraps of flowery trims
Tracing paper
Dressmaker's carbon paper
Matching sewing thread

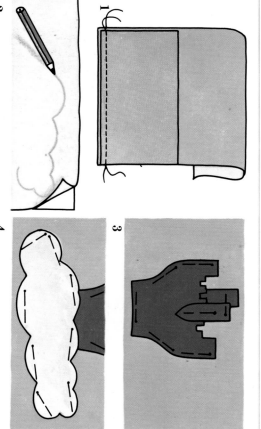

from light blue poplin cut out a piece 41 × 32in.

□ Place base and top pieces with right sides together, matching one 32in long edge. Pin, baste and stitch together along this edge, taking ⅜in seam allowance. Press seam open (fig. 1).

□ Trace the appliqué patterns from trace patterns on pages 103-105, allowing ⅜in extra where shown for appliqué overlap (fig. 2). Cut each piece in the appropriate fabric the number of times stated, omitting the leaves.

□ Position the castle on the background fabric, first adding the towers and then the turrets in numbered order. Pin in place (fig. 3).

□ From fur fabric, cut out one cloud shape, 15in long, 6¼in deep. Pin centrally onto the background fabric, over-lapping castle base (fig. 4).

□ From brown cord fabric cut out a path 21cm long, curving it as shown (fig. 5). Pin it in position on the background fabric.

□ For the background of the lower half of the picture, from green poplin cut out a piece 32 × 15½in. For top of picture,

□ Position the cottage walls on the background fabric, overlapping path. Pin them firmly in place.

□ From pale brown cotton fabric cut out three 1¾in squares for window panes. Using dark brown thread, sew diagonal lines of stitching across each square of fabric to represent leaded panes (fig. 6). Place the panes behind the window frames, trimming if necessary, and position them on cottage. Pin them firmly in place. Position door on cottage and pin in place (fig. 7).

□ Position both roof pieces on top of cottage, overlapping walls. Pin in place.

□ From dark green corduroy cut a bush 9in long, 4¾in high. Pin it on background, overlapping cottage.

□ Sew two lines of gray close zig-zag stitch to represent smoke (fig. 8).

□ Position the beanstalk root on background fabric. Pin it in place.

□ Baste and stitch around each appliqué piece, close to the outer edge, using matching sewing thread. Using close zig-zag stitch, work around each appliqué piece again, over existing stitching, with matching thread (fig. 9).

□ Cut out 25 green leaves, varying the shapes by turning the patterns both ways and using different fabrics.

□ Select four leaves to serve as pockets. On each, finish the top edge by working

102

Trace pattern

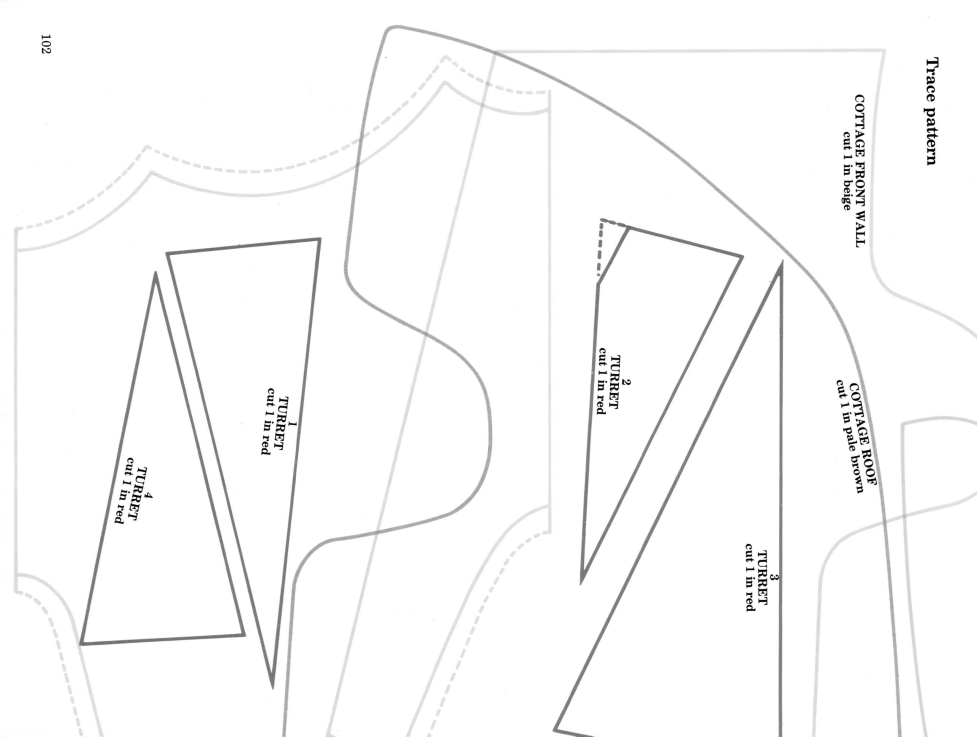

COTTAGE FRONT WALL
cut 1 in beige

COTTAGE ROOF
cut 1 in pale brown

COTTAGE SIDE ROOF
cut 1 in pale brown

1
TURRET
cut 1 in red

2
TURRET
cut 1 in red

3
TURRET
cut 1 in red

4
TURRET
cut 1 in red

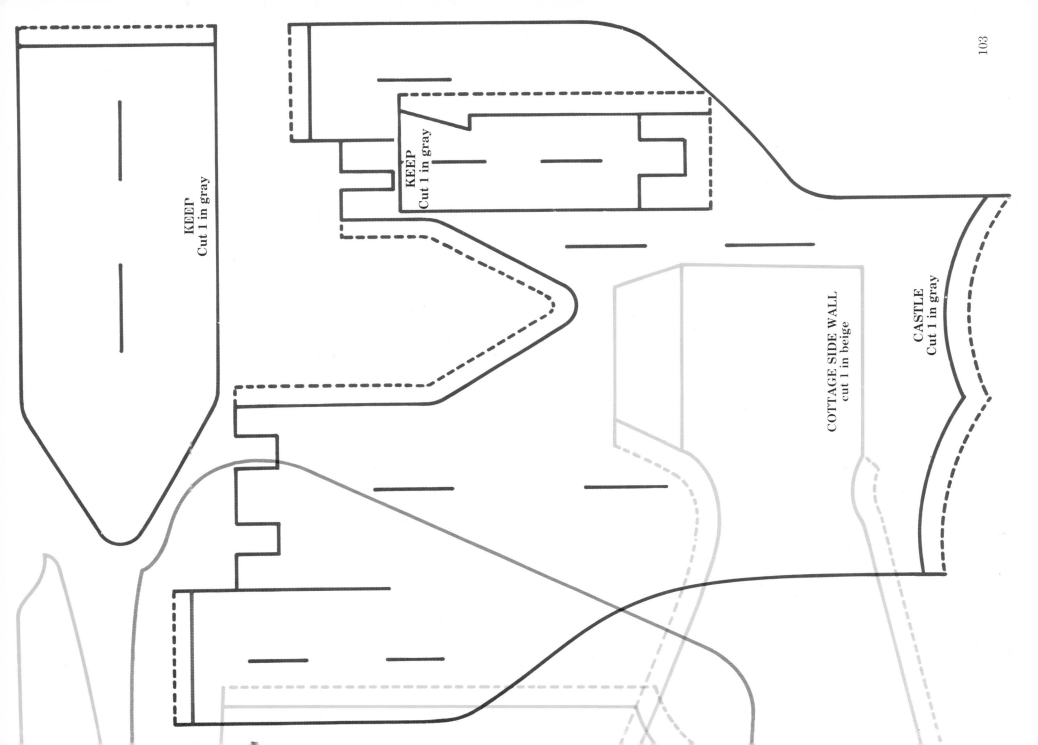

KEEP
Cut 1 in gray

KEEP
Cut 1 in gray

COTTAGE SIDE WALL
cut 1 in beige

CASTLE
Cut 1 in gray

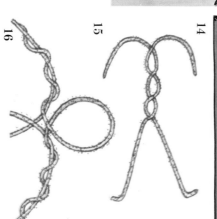
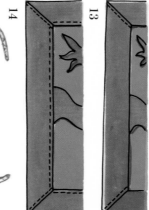

close zig-zag stitch along the edge for about 2in, between marks (fig. 10).

□Baste a curved line from the bean-stalk root up to the top of the picture as a guide for placing the leaves. Pin, baste and stitch the leaves in place on the background, in the same way as the other appliqué pieces, leaving each edge open so leaves form pockets (fig. 11). Stitch pocket leaves at intervals up stalk. Remove basting.

□Decorate the cottage. Cut trim to represent flowers; pin, baste and stitch

in position along the base of the cottage (fig. 12). Pin, baste and stitch trim around the door and up the side wall of the cottage. Stitch bead to the cottage door for handle. Cut trim into flower heads. Pin, baste and stitch flower heads to bush.

□Press picture from wrong side.

□For the border, from red poplin cut out two strips each 66½in × 7½in and two strips each 43½in × 7½in.

□Pin, baste and stitch long border strips to either side of picture, match-

ing long edges and taking ¾in seams (fig. 13). Press strips away from picture. Pin, baste and stitch short strips to top and base of picture in the same way.

□Lay the picture border flat. Fold in and miter each corner from the right side. Pin, baste and stitch down each miter corner (fig. 14). Trim away surplus fabric.

□For backing, from light blue poplin cut out one piece 66 × 43in. Position backing on picture/border, right sides together, matching all outer edges. Pin, baste and stitch all around, leaving 10in opening in the base edge. Trim corners and seams and turn quilt right side out.

□Cut out two pieces of batting each 65 × 42in. Place batting pieces together, matching all edges. Secure together with large basting stitches. Insert batting into quilt. Turn in opening edges and slipstitch together to close.

□Lay the quilt flat. Pin, baste and stitch around inner edge of border, through all thicknesses, securing the batting in position (fig. 15).

Jack

Finished size
6in tall

Materials
Three pipe cleaners
Scraps of flesh-colored felt
Embroidery floss for features
Scrap of doll's hair or fine yarn
5in square of cotton fabric for clothes
Scraps of blue and orange felt for clothes
One small feather
Fabric glue
Scrap of stuffing
Matching sewing thread

□Twist two pipe cleaners together, 3in from one end. Open out the remainder and bend out for shoulders and arms. Turn up ½in at opposite ends for feet (fig. 16).

□Using the other pipe cleaner, twist the center into a circle for the head, twisting the remaining ends around the top of the arms (fig. 17).

Trace pattern

□Cut out two circles of flesh-colored felt for the head. Place one circle on each side of pipe cleaner head and overcast together, stuffing as you work.

□Embroider the features on one side of the head. Stick the hair in position.

□ Cut narrow strips of flesh-colored felt to cover arms and legs. Fold each strip in half over pipe cleaner limbs; stitch in place, with tiny seam allowance.
□ Pad body with stuffing; secure in position by winding thread around body.
□ For shirt, fold the fabric square in half. Place Jack on fabric with fold at top. Cut out a T shape, curving the underarm seams. Pin, baste and stitch the underarm seam, taking a tiny seam allowance. Slit down the center back of the shirt. Place the shirt on Jack. Run lines of gathering around the wrists and secure. Lap over the back opening and stitch in position.
□ Cut out two 1½in squares of blue felt for pants. Fold each square in half for pants legs. Stitch up long edges for ½in taking a tiny seam allowance. Slip each leg on Jack and overcast pants together at back and front.
□ For vest cut out an oblong of orange felt 2¾ × 1¾in. Cut out two armholes ½in in from long edges. Stitch shoulder seams. Curve lower front edges. Sew vest on Jack.
□ For hat cut out a 2½in diameter circle for brim. Cut out the center of the circle to fit Jack's head. Cut out another circle ¾in diameter for hat crown. Cut a length of felt ½in wide and overcast between brim and crown, trimming felt to fit. Add a thin strip of orange felt and the feather to decorate the hat. Glue it on Jack's head.

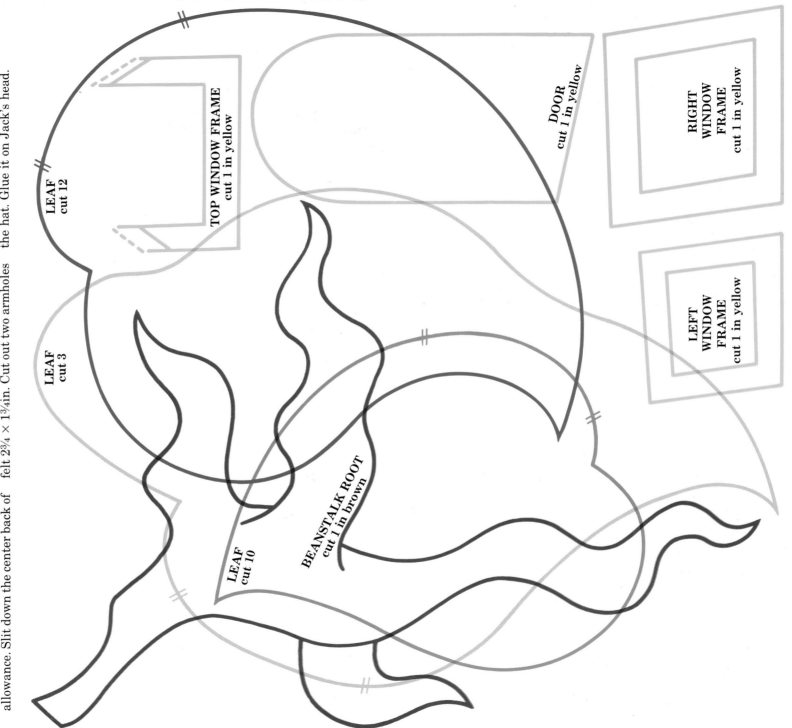

LEAF
cut 12

LEAF
cut 3

LEAF
cut 10

BEANSTALK ROOT
cut 1 in brown

TOP WINDOW FRAME
cut 1 in yellow

DOOR
cut 1 in yellow

LEFT
WINDOW
FRAME
cut 1 in yellow

RIGHT
WINDOW
FRAME
cut 1 in yellow

Animal Sleeping Bags

Children will really look forward to bedtime when they can slip into these warm and cuddly sleeping bags!

Mr Rabbit

Finished size
About 65in long, 26in wide

Materials
4yd of 36in-wide solid color cotton print fabric

2¾yd of 36in-wide solid color cotton fabric for lining

2¾yd of 36in-wide soft cotton such as chambray or gauze for interlining

2¾yd of 36in-wide medium-weight polyester batting

¾yd of 48in-wide fleece fabric

Mr Rabbit

12in square of pink felt
Scraps of light and dark brown felt
Tracing paper
Matching and contrasting sewing thread

□Using tracing paper and a sharp pencil trace pattern pieces for rabbit shown on pages 110–111. Cut out each pattern piece.

□To make pattern for tail, from tracing paper cut out a rectangle 8 × 4¾in. Fold paper in half widthwise. Mark a curve on the pattern from fold to side edge (fig. 1). Cut along curved line. Open out.

□From print fabric cut out four paws and four legs. From fleece cut two heads, two ears and two tails. From pink felt cut two ears. Cut one tail and two ears from batting. Cut eyes from brown felt.

□For main sleeping bag/body cut out two pieces each 50 × 27½in, from cotton print fabric. Cut out two pieces the same size from batting, interlining and cotton lining.

□For front body, position one batting piece and then one interlining piece on wrong side of one fabric body, with all outer edges even. Pin and baste together all around outer edges, and across fabric at intervals (fig. 2).

□Quilt across the front body with lines of stitching, the first line 6¾in from one short edge – the top – and the remaining lines 6in apart (fig. 3). Make and quilt back body in the same way.

□Place two fabric paws with right sides together, with all outer edges even. Place one batting paw to one side of fabric paws, matching all outer edges. Pin, baste and stitch around the paw, leaving straight edges open (fig. 4). Trim seam allowance. Turn paw right side out.

□Mark the claws on the paw with three lines of topstitching using a contrasting sewing thread (fig. 5). Make the second paw in the same way. Make the legs in the same way, adding leg markings.

□Place tails with right sides together with all outer edges even. Place batting tail on one side of fabric tails, matching outer edges. Pin, baste and stitch around the tail, leaving straight edges open (fig. 6). Trim seam allowance and turn tail right side out.

□Place paws on right side of front body, facing inward on each side, 1½in down from top edge, raw edges even. Pin and baste paws in place.

□Place legs on right side of front body, facing inward, with heels 1in up from lower edge and long raw edges even. Pin and baste the legs in place. Place tail on right side of front body, centered on lower edge and pointing inward, raw edges even. Pin and baste in place (fig. 8).

☐ Place back body on right side of front body. Pin, baste and stitch all around body, leaving top edge open and catching in paws, legs and tail. Trim seam allowances and corners. Turn body right side out.

☐ Place one felt ear to one fleece ear with right sides together. Place one batting ear to one side of fabric ears. Pin, baste and stitch together all around, leaving lower straight edge open. Trim and turn ear right side out (fig. 9). Make the second ear in the same way as you made the first one.

☐ Lightly draw the features onto one fabric head – this will be the front.

☐ Position the two inner eyes on the two outer eyes; pin and baste. Position eyes on front head over marked pencil eyes. Pin, baste and stitch combined eyes in place (fig. 10).

☐ Place two batting heads behind front head; pin and baste in position. Pin, baste and topstitch marked features using matching thread for eyes and contrasting sewing thread for nose and mouth.

☐ Position ears on front head in marked positions. Place ears facing inward with raw edges even. Pin and baste in place (fig. 11).

☐ Place back head with right side to front head. Pin, baste and stitch all around head, catching in ears and leaving neck edge open. Trim seam and turn head right side out.

☐ Position head centrally on top edge of back body with back of head against right side of quilted fabric, so front head will face toward the front. Baste head in place (fig. 12).

☐ Place lining body pieces with right sides together with, all the outer edges even. Now pin, baste and stitch the side edges of the lining pieces.

☐ With right sides together, place lining body over body, matching side seams and raw edges. Pin, baste and stitch around top edge, catching in head at the back (fig. 13).

☐ Pull lining up. Turn in lower raw edges and pin, baste and stitch across lower edge.

☐ Push lining inside main bag and catch together at the bottom corners of the sleeping bag.

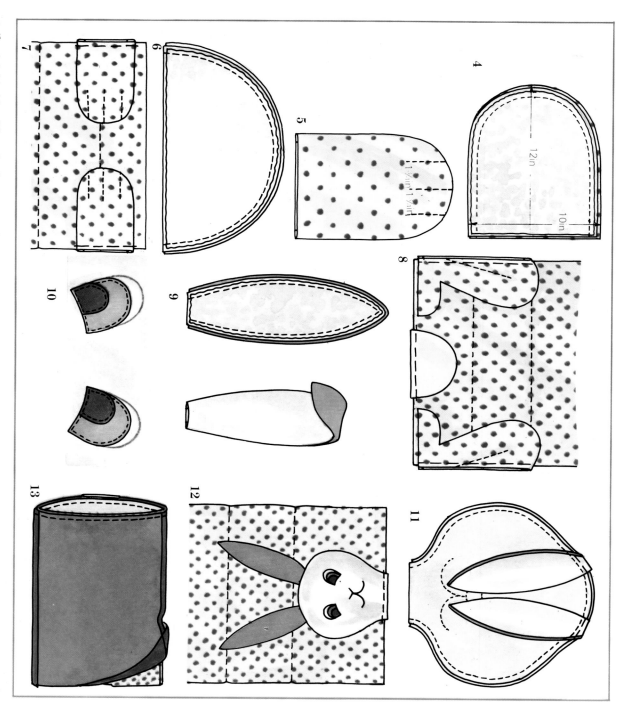

Mr Fox

Finished size

About 65 × 26in

Materials

4yd of 36in-wide cotton print fabric

2¾yd of 36in-wide solid color cotton fabric for lining

2¾yd of 36in-wide soft cotton such as chambray or gauze for interlining

2¾yd of 36in-wide medium-weight polyester batting

¾yd of 48in-wide fleece fabric

Scraps of green and brown felt

Length of brown yarn

Tracing paper

Matching and contrasting sewing thread

□ Trace and cut out pattern pieces as for Mr Rabbit.

□ For bib front, on tracing paper draw a line 16in long and mark the center. Draw a line 24in long at a right angle to the center point. Join the top of the center line to the outside points to form a triangle (fig.1).

□ For a main tail piece, on tracing paper draw a line 3½in long and mark the center. Draw a line 17in long at a right angle from the center point. Mark 4in on either side of top of line. Join the outside lines to form the main tail piece (fig.2).

□ For tail tip, on tracing paper draw a line 8in long and mark the center point. Draw a line 6¾in long at a right angle to center point. Join the top of center line to outside points to form a triangle (fig.4).

□ For tail pattern, place main tail on tracing paper. Place tail tip pattern against it, allowing for seam allowance. Draw around it and cut out (fig.4).

□ From cotton print fabric cut out two heads, four outer ears, four paws, four legs and two main tail pieces. Cut one bib front, two inner ears and two outer eyes and two tail tips from fleece. From batting cut out one tail piece and two ears. From green felt cut two inner eyes. From brown felt cut one nose and two eye highlights.

□ Cut out and quilt front and back body pieces as for Mr Rabbit.

□ Position bib front centrally on body front, matching top edges. Pin, baste and zig-zag stitch bib in place (fig.5).

□ Make paws and legs as for Mr Rabbit.

□ Place one main tail on one tail tip, matching straight raw edges. Pin, baste and stitch together. Repeat, to make second side of tail.

□ Place tails with right sides together, matching outer edges and tail tip seams. Place batting tail to wrong side of fabric tails, matching outer edges. Pin, baste and stitch all around, leaving top edge open. Trim and turn tail right side out.

□ Position paws, legs and tail and join body pieces as for Mr Rabbit.

□ Place two inner ears centrally on outer ears; pin, baste and zig-zag stitch in position. Place one combined ear to one plain ear, with right sides together matching all outer edges. Place one batting ear to one side of fabric ears, matching all outer edges. Pin, baste and stitch all around, leaving straight edge open. Trim and turn ear right side out. Make second ear in the same way.

□ Make head and complete Mr Fox, stitching nose outline in brown yarn.

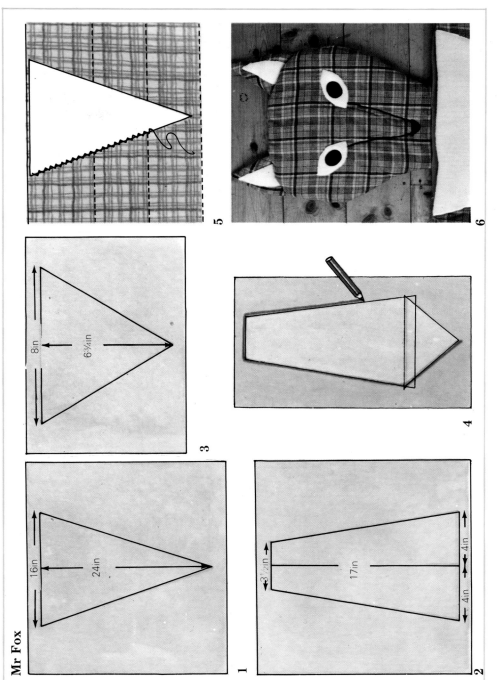

1

2

3

4

5

6

Trace patterns
¾in seam allowances included

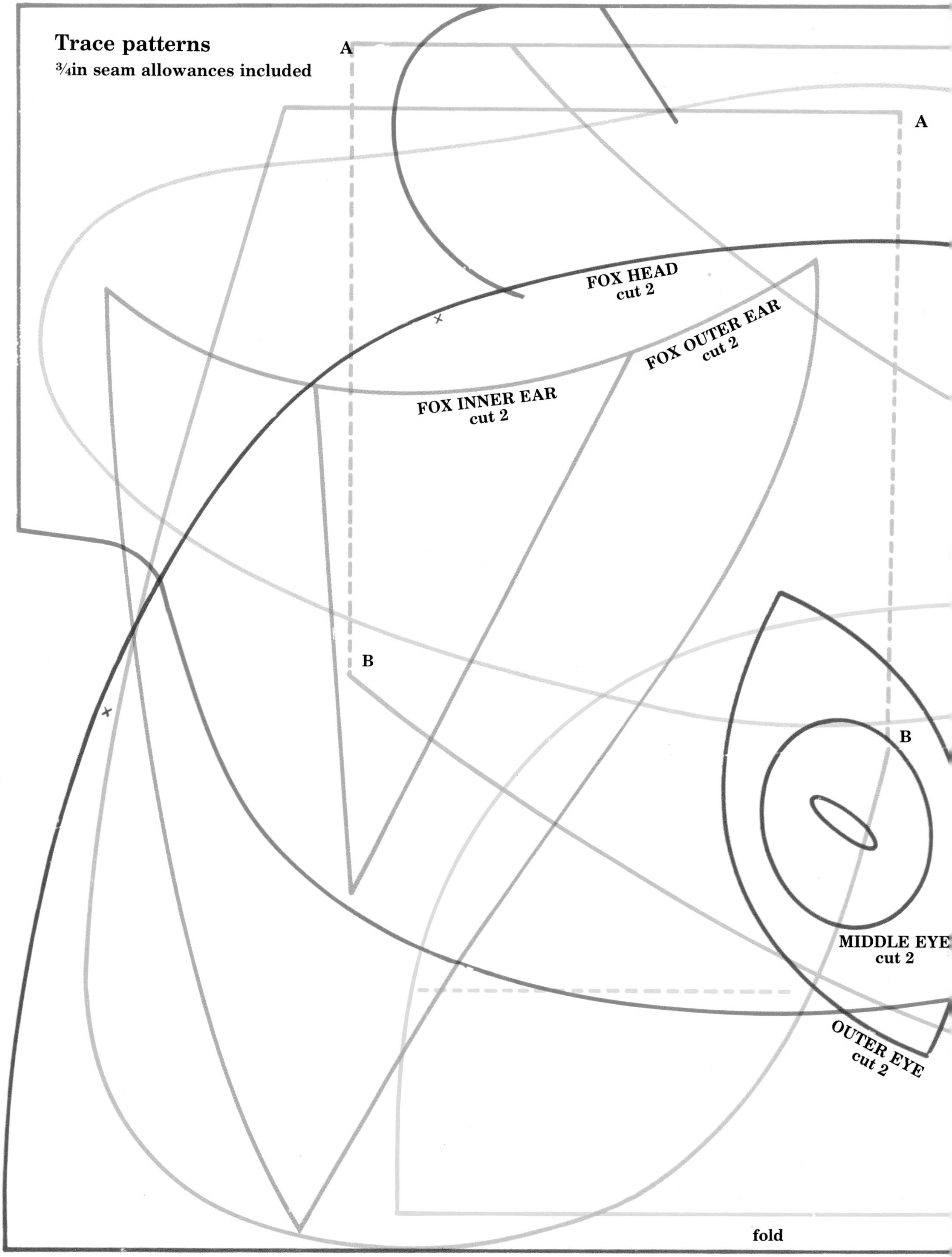

A

B

FOX INNER EAR
cut 2

FOX HEAD
cut 2

FOX OUTER EAR
cut 2

OUTER EYE
cut 2

MIDDLE EYE
cut 2

B

A

fold

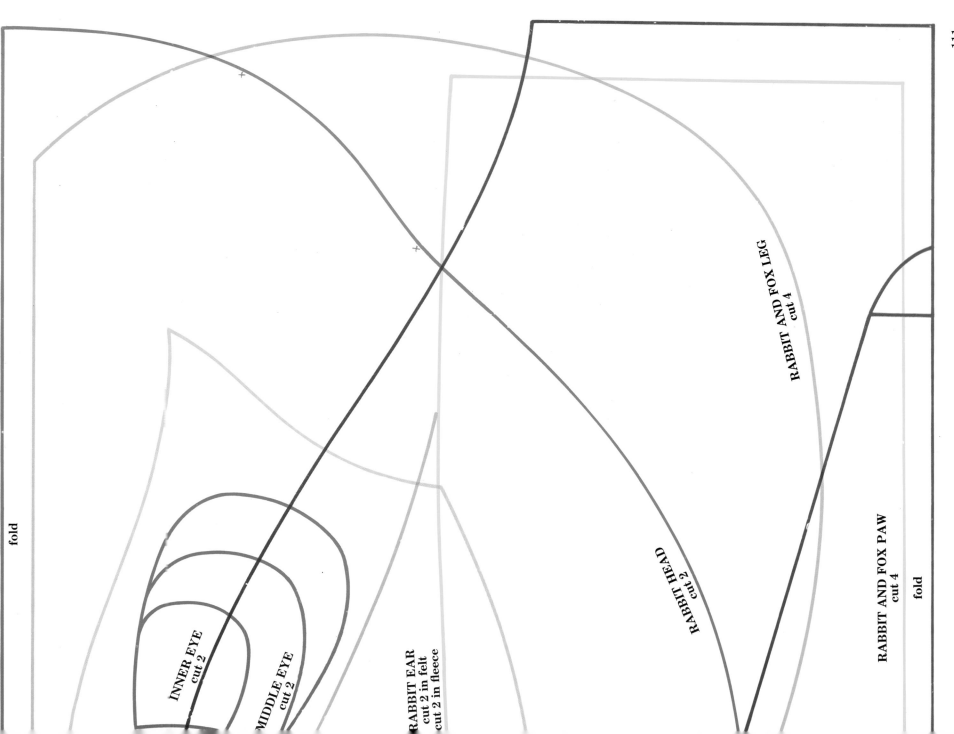

INNER EYE
cut 2

MIDDLE EYE
cut 2

RABBIT EAR
cut 2 in felt
cut 2 in fleece

RABBIT HEAD
cut 2

RABBIT AND FOX LEG
cut 4

RABBIT AND FOX PAW
cut 4

fold

fold

fold

Monogrammed Towels and Pillowcases

Give that touch of class to your personal belongings with monograms, worked by hand or by machine. We have provided alphabets in two different styles – choose the one that best suits the article you are decorating.

Materials

Garment or household item which lends itself to this kind of decoration

Stranded embroidery floss

Sewing thread

Tracing paper

Dressmaker's carbon paper

Embroidery hoop

Note Complete alphabets for the towels, in Roman (as shown) and script, are given on pages 114–15, together with instructions for enlarging the letters.

For the initials on the lace-trimmed pillowcases, see the alphabet on page 116, from which the letters must be traced to size.

Pillowcases

□We have embroidered lace-trimmed pillowcases for a Victorian look, but the design is just as effective on more modern looking solid-color cases with the embroidery done in a contrasting color. Also, we have centered the letters, but there is no reason why they cannot be placed along the outside edge or to a corner.

Preparing the pillowcase

□Mark the vertical center line (fig. 1) and measure 5½in down this line from the top edge: mark a short line across and at right angles to the center line. Use this line as the base line when transferring the monogram.

□Transfer the letters onto the fabric,

taking care to position them the right way up. Pin a piece of iron-on interfacing to the back of the fabric underneath the letters and baste in place. Stretch the fabric in an embroidery hoop.

Embroidering the letters

□Using three strands of embroidery floss, work stem stitch along the single lines of the letters and split stitch on the double lines. Make two rows of running stitch between the rows of split stitch (fig. 2).

□Make the first satin stitch at a 45° angle across the widest part of the letter and work all subsequent stitches first to one side and then to the other.

Note On curved areas the satin stitches may be closer together on one side

than on the other so as to fit into the curve.

□Work the flower stems in stem stitch and outline the leaves and flowers in split stitch. Fill in the leaves with satin stitch worked diagonally. To fill in the flowers, work satin stitch from the edge inwards, and finish the center with a French knot (fig. 3).

□Remove the fabric from the embroidery hoop and carefully cut away the excess interfacing (fig. 4). Place right side down over a pad and press.

Towels

□Choose three initials for this monogram and enlarge them to a suitable size, following the instructions. The

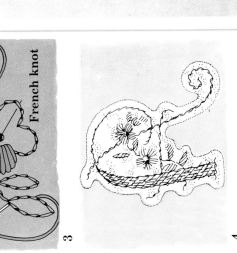

Pillowcases

5½in

2in
¼in
⅜in
(Lace)

Centre line

1

Stem stitch

Split stitch

2 Running stitch

Satin stitch

French knot

3

4

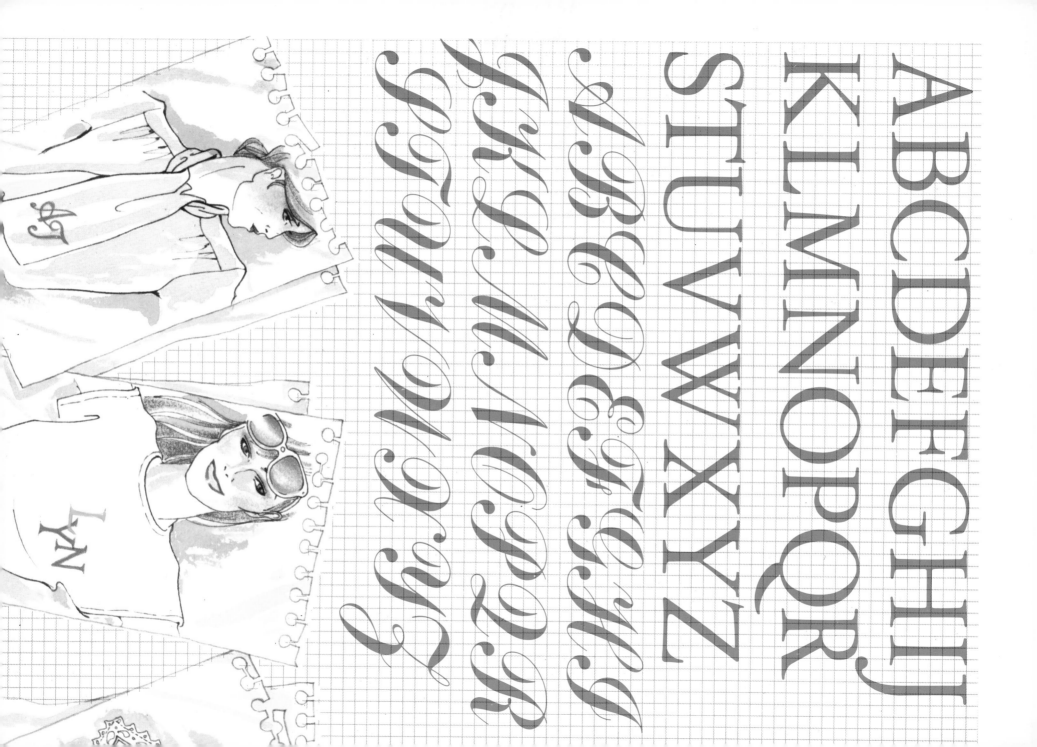

initial of the last name should be larger than the others. Trace the letters.

□ Using dressmaker's carbon paper, transfer the three letters centrally onto the towel, above the edging, placing the larger letter in the center as shown.

□ These letters are sewn in satin stitch by machine, using ordinary sewing thread. Before you stitch the initials, practice the stitching on a spare piece of fabric (preferably an old towel) until you achieve the desired effect.

□ Set the machine to satin stitch or closed zig-zag stitch. Carefully stitch along the letters from top to bottom, beginning with the narrower parts of the letters. Increase the width of the stitch slightly for the thicker parts. Tie off all the loose ends on the back.

□ Repeat for the second towel.

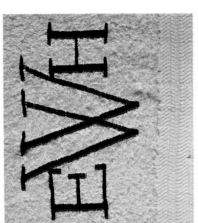

To enlarge the initials

The letters shown here are about 3/4in high, but can be enlarged to any size.

□ *There is a grid of 1/8in squares over the letters on this page. To make them larger, take a sheet of paper and – using a ruler – draw a square grid to the size you require. For example, for letters four times the original, the grid squares must be four times larger.*

□ *Copy the letters onto your enlarged grid, positioning each part of the letter on the square corresponding to the equivalent square on the original grid.*

Appliqué Towels

In virtually no time at all you can create beautiful designer towels – for your own linen closet or for that special present. Machine-appliqué is quick and easy or, for a more traditional look why not embroider the motifs by hand!

Materials

Set of 4 towels – we used 2 guest towels and 2 hand towels in 2 complementary shades of green (but any size will do)
Small amount of light and dark green satin
Small amount of floral print cotton fabric, such as lawn
Matching light and dark green sewing thread
Tracing paper
Thin cardboard for pattern
Soft pencil or tailor's chalk

Trace pattern

☐ Trace the leaf and flower shapes on thin cardboard. Cut these out and draw around them on the appropriate fabrics (fig. 1). For each towel cut 1 flower and 2 leaves.

☐ Draw the veins on the leaves, using chalk or a pencil (fig. 2).

☐ Use the design plan as a guide to place leaf no.1 in the correct position. Pin and baste the shapes to the towel. With a small straight stitch, machine stitch around the leaf, keeping close to the raw edge. Begin stitching from the base of the leaf, which will be covered by the flower. Reset the sewing machine to satin stitch or closed zig-zag stitch (width 3 or 4, minimum length) and carefully stitch along edge of leaf, covering raw edge (fig. 3).

☐ Work the central rib and two veins of the leaf in satin stitch, varying the stitch width if desired (fig. 4).

☐ Repeat for the second leaf (fig. 5).

☐ Stitch the flower in position in the same way, using a thread contrasting with that used for the leaves (fig. 6).

☐ Finally, using tailor's chalk draw the 2 stems on the towel, using the design plan as a guide. (You can use the side of a plate as a guide in drawing the curves.) Work the two stems in satin stitch as for the central vein of the leaves, using contrasting thread.

☐ Press the towels gently on the wrong side to make the stitching stand out.

Hand-sewn appliqué

If your sewing machine does not do zig-zag stitch you can decorate your towels the same way, using hand stitching.

☐ Before cutting out shapes, machine stitch along the drawn outline of the shape. This helps to give a smoothly turned-under edge (fig. 1). Cut out shapes, adding ¼in outside the stitching line for seam allowances (fig. 2).

☐ Clip the seam allowance. Turn under the seam allowance, concealing the stitching, baste and press (fig. 3).

☐ Baste the shapes in position on the towel. Apply each shape to the towel using a fine slip-stitch (fig. 4).

☐ Using a contrasting stranded embroidery floss, stitch around each shape, using a close blanket stitch (fig. 5).

☐ Work stems and veins of leaves, using satin stitch (fig. 6) or couching.

☐ To sew couching, lay several threads along the line; then, using a single thread, secure the couching threads with a tiny stitch at ⅜in intervals (fig. 7).

Leaf shape 1 (work first)

Leaf shape 2 (work second)

Flower shape (work last)

Lay in position, pin, tack and stitch.

Machine appliqué

1

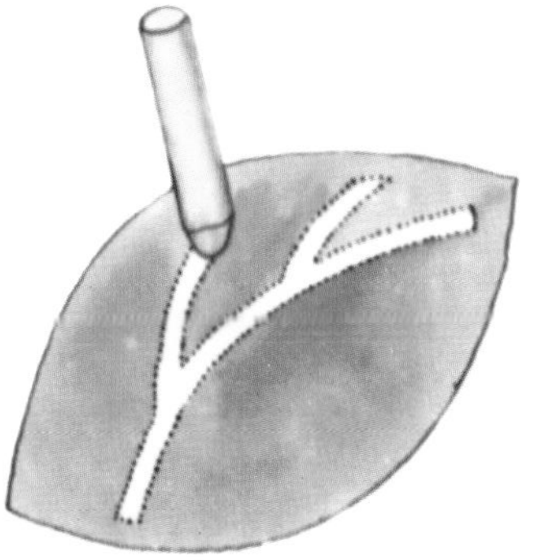

2

3

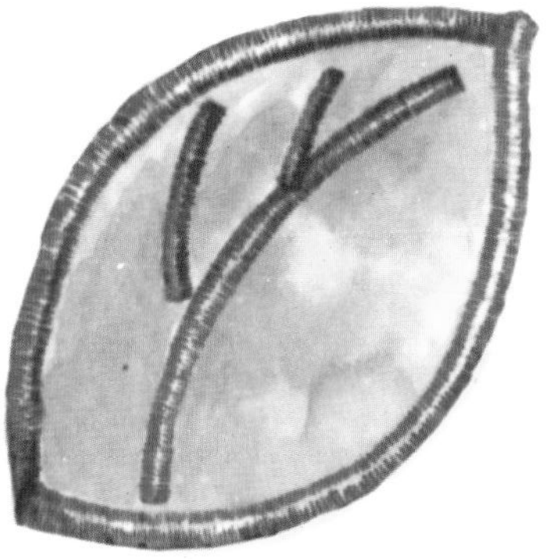

4

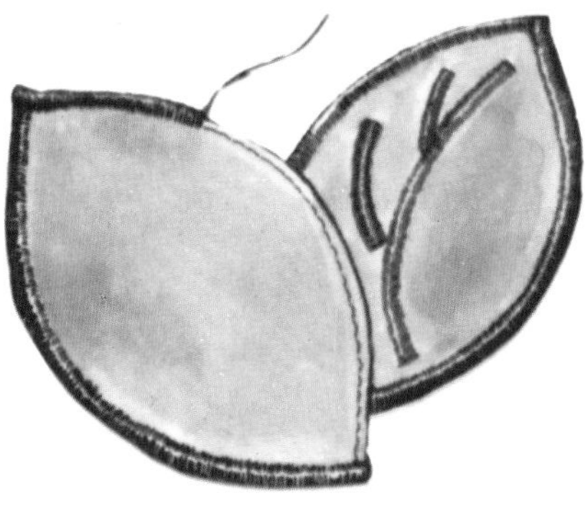

5

6

Hand-sewn appliqué

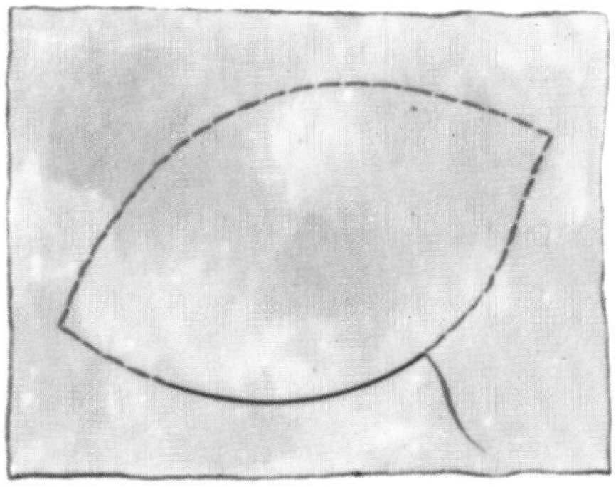

1

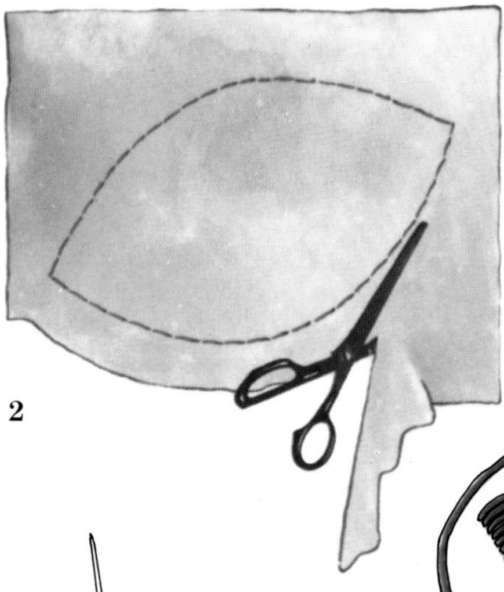

2

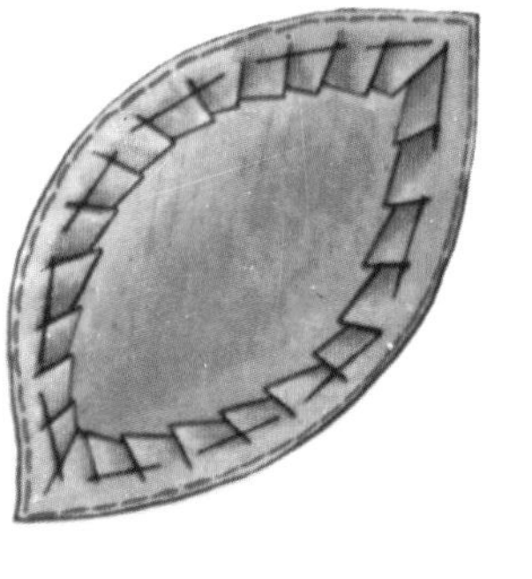

3

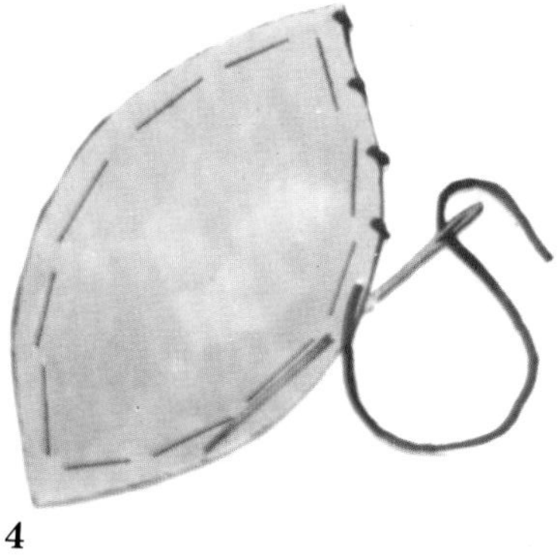

4

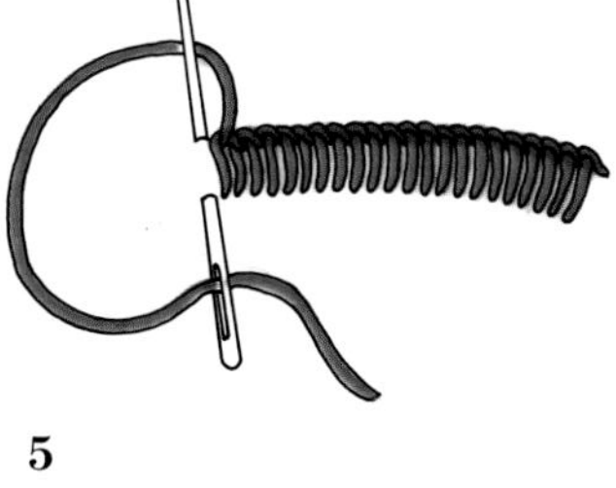

5

6

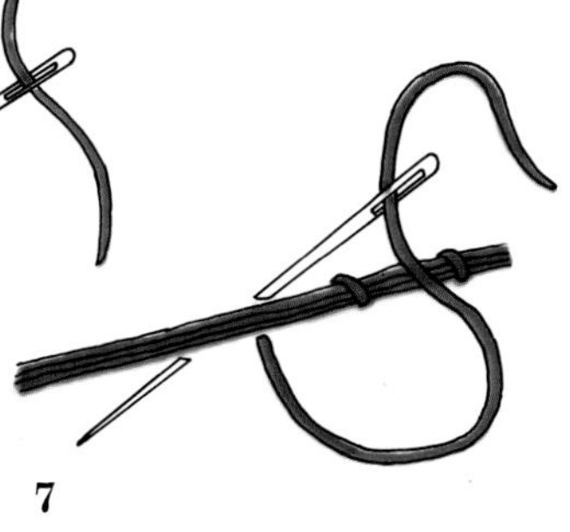

7

Rainbow Bath Mat

Step out of the tub into the comfort of this colorful mat. Just make pompons in a brightly colored synthetic yarn and stitch in rows to a fabric base.

Finished size
About 28in long by 19in wide

Materials
120yds of acrylic yarn in each of the eight colors
7/8yd of 36in-wide fabric or fine canvas for backing
7/8yd of 36in-wide heavyweight iron-on interfacing
Large bodkin
Piece of cardboard 7 × 4in
Thread to match backing fabric

Note *This yarn comes in hanks, so you will have to work out how many to buy to obtain the yardage you need.*

☐ On cardboard, mark two 3in diameter circles. Cut out each circle carefully (fig. 1).

☐ In the center of each circle mark a smaller circle with ¾in diameter. Cut out each center circle carefully and discard, leaving two rings (fig. 2).

☐ Cut first ball of yarn into four 6½yd lengths. Thread one length of yarn onto the bodkin (fig. 3).

☐ Place both cardboard ring patterns together. Thread the long end of yarn through the center hole of the pattern. Hold the yarn end firmly in place and take the yarn over the outer part of the pattern and up through the center hole again (fig. 4).

☐ Continue winding the yarn around and around the cardboard in the same way (fig. 5), covering it evenly until the yarn is used and the cardboard is covered.

☐ Cut a 6in length of matching yarn for binding. Cut through the outer edge of

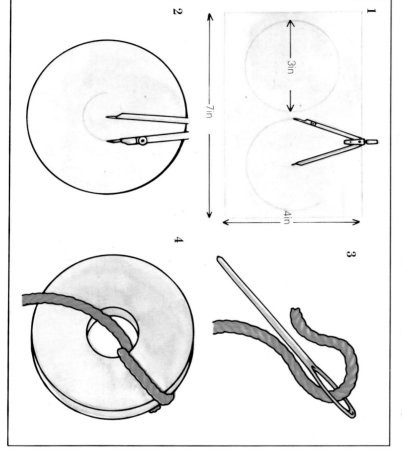

1

2

3

4

3in

7in

4in

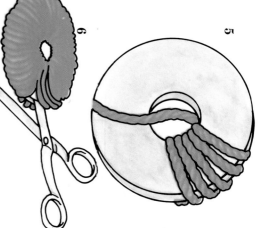

7

6

5

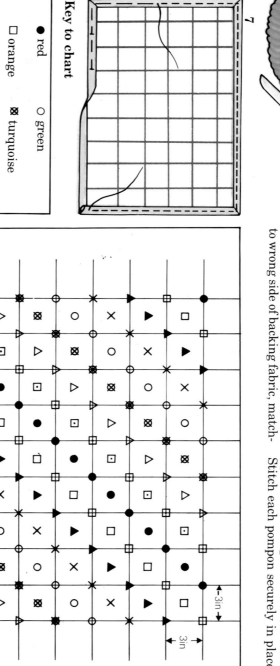

the yarn between the two circles of cardboard (fig. 6). Slip the 6in length of yarn between the two circles and wind it tightly around all the yarn where it passes through the center of the pattern and secure.

☐Make 16 pompons in each of the colors, except for the two colors at each end of the range. Make 14 pompons in these two colors.

☐From backing fabric cut out one piece for backing 29½in × 20½in. From interfacing cut out one piece also 29½ × 20½in.

☐Place the interfacing with shiny side to wrong side of backing fabric, match-

ing all outer edges. Press the interfacing in place.

☐Using a pencil and a ruler mark 3in squares across interfaced side of fabric. Mark squares from center outward, leaving 1½in margin all around.

☐On backing fabric, turn under a double ½in-wide hem all around, mitering the corners. Pin, baste and stitch in place all around (fig. 7).

☐Stitch the pompons onto the interfaced side of the backing fabric. Position a pompon at each of the pencil intersections and in the center of each square, following the chart for colors. Stitch each pompon securely in place.

Crochet Bath Mat

This mat is just the thing for catching splashes and drips. It is made in thick cotton yarn in a sturdy basket weave pattern and is trimmed around three sides with a short fringe.

Finished size
16½in wide by 27in long, excluding fringe

Materials
700yd of thick, white craft cotton yarn
Size E crochet hook

Gauge
1 patt rep (12sts) to 2½in and 16 rows to 5in in patt on E hook.

Note *If your bathroom floor is smooth, it may be wise to add some form of non-slip back to the mat.*

Crochet pattern
Using E hook make 140ch.
Base row 1dc into 4th ch from hook. 1dc into each ch to end. Turn. Commence patt.
1st row (RS) 2ch, work *around* each of next 5dc by working yo, insert hook from front to back between next 2dc, around dc at left and through work from back to front; draw yarn through and complete dc in usual way – called double chain around front (dc around Ft), work *around* each of next 6dc by working yo, insert hook from back to front between next 2dc, around dc at left and through work from front to back; draw yarn through and complete dc in usual way – called 1 double crochet around back (dc around Bk), now work 6dc * around Ft, 6dc around Bk, rep from * to within last 6sts, dc around Ft to end. Turn.
2nd row 2ch, work 5dc around Bk, 6dc around Ft, * 6dc around Bk, 6dc around Ft, rep from * to within last 6sts, dc around Bk to end. Turn.
3rd row As first row.
4th row As first row.
5th row As 2nd row.
6th row As first row.
These 6 rows form the patt. Rep them 7 times more, then work first to 3rd rows again.
Fasten off.

Fringe
□ Using four strands of yarn together, knot fringe into every alternate row end along each short edge and into every alternate st along one long edge.
□ Trim the ends neatly and evenly to the desired length.

Chapter 4

Table linen

Circular tablecloth

Embroidered tablecloth

Cherry blossom tablecloth

Cutwork tablecloth

Patchwork place mats and napkins

Quilted place mats and napkins

Circular Tablecloth

A set of coordinating tablecloths in fresh, modern fabrics will brighten up your décor and give an old table a new lease of life. Here a floor-length ruffled cloth has been covered with a short round cloth in a floral print.

A circular cloth requires a simple pattern and, unless your table is very small, lengths of fabric will have to be joined. The joins should be made at each side of the cloth.

A short cloth can be made from a plain circle of fabric with the overhang 12–15in long; this type of cloth is particularly suitable for a dining table. A floor-length cloth can be made either in the same way, or from a central panel that fits the table top with a floor-length gathered ruffle or skirt. This is more suitable for a side table or as a decorative design feature in a room, but less practical for everyday use. It may be used with a smaller cloth in toning or contrasting fabric placed over the top of the gathered cloth.

Choosing the fabric

Cotton and linen are good, hard-wearing fabrics, which hang well and have the crisp finish required for a decorative and lasting tablecloth.

When considering day-to-day care and laundering, a synthetic fabric or a cotton/polyester blend is more practical. If a synthetic fabric is used, it must be of reasonable weight to hang well.

Solid color or patterned fabrics are equally suitable, and a combination of both can be used for a set of two cloths. If a patterned fabric is used for a ruffled cloth, make sure that it can be used sideways, as the width of the fabric will be the depth of the ruffle.

Do not choose a large design if your table is small – as a general rule, match the scale of the pattern to the size of the table for which the cloth is intended.

If desired, plain fabric can be decorated with, for example, appliqué or embroidery.

Various edgings may be used to finish the cloth in a decorative way.

The simplest is to bind the raw edge with bias binding, or to add fringe. A short gathered ruffle will look attractive on the edge of a cloth: make it twice the length of the cloth's circumference.

A scalloped edge is pretty also: a round pattern is used for tracing the scallops onto the fabric, and the outline is machine stitched with a close zigzag. The surplus fabric is trimmed away close to the stitching.

Appliqué looks effective around the edge of a short cloth, particularly with the motif repeated in the center.

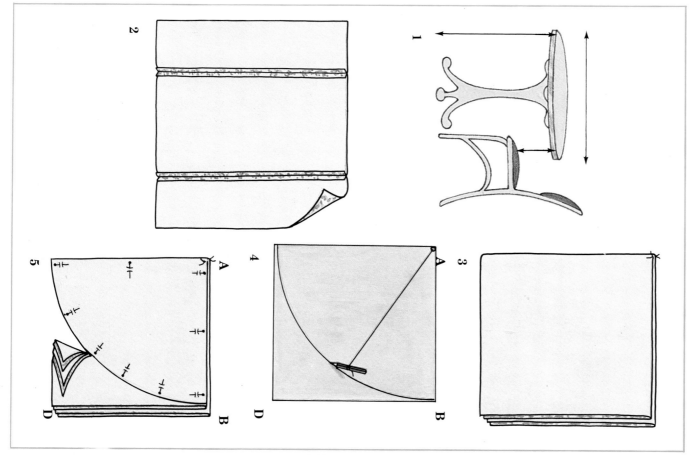

126

The plain round tablecloth

Finished size
Tablecloth 2¼yd in diameter

Materials
4½yd of 48in-wide fabric (if the fabric has a large design, add one extra pattern repeat)
7yd bias binding for edging (or ½yd plain fabric)
Matching sewing thread
Paper for pattern
A piece of string and a pencil

Measure the diameter of the table, then decide how much overhang you want. For a short cloth, measure from the top of the table to a chair seat; for a long cloth, measure to the floor (fig. 1). Multiply the overhang by two and add to the diameter of the table. This will give you the diameter of the finished tablecloth.

If the diameter is less than the width of your selected fabric, one length of fabric is enough. However, if the diameter is wider, you will need to join two or more lengths of fabric. If the fabric has a large design, also allow one extra pattern repeat per extra length of fabric for matching.

Making the tablecloth
□Starting with a straight edge, cut one length of fabric, the same length as the diameter of the finished cloth. Cut the remaining fabric in half lengthwise. Join one strip to each side of the first length, taking a ⅝in-wide seam allowance and taking care to match the pattern: pin, baste and machine stitch together. Cut the strips level with the first length of fabric. Trim seam allowances to ⅜in and finish the raw edges (fig. 2).
□Fold the fabric in half, right sides together, and fold it in half again. Mark the corner which is the center of the fabric with a tailor's tack (fig. 3).
□Cut a square of paper, the same size as the folded fabric. Take a piece of string and tie one end around a pin and the other end around a pencil: the distance between the pin and the pencil should equal the radius of the tablecloth. Put the pin at corner A of the paper square and, holding the pencil at a right angle to the paper, draw an arc from corner B to corner C. Cut out the pattern (fig. 4).
□Place the pattern on the folded fabric so that corner A is on top of the tailor's tack. Pin and cut out along the curved

line of the pattern from C to B (fig. 5).
□Remove the pattern and unfold the fabric. Apply bias binding to finish the edge of the cloth.

The floor-length cloth

Finished size
Tablecloth 48in in diameter with a full, 30in deep ruffle

Materials
12yd of 48in-wide fabric
10¼yd bias binding for edging (or ½yd plain fabric)
Matching sewing thread
Paper for pattern

To calculate the length of fabric required for the ruffle, measure the circumference of the table. For a fairly full ruffle, allow twice this measurement. If less fullness is required, 1½ times is enough. Also add 1¼in for seam allowances. This measurement will also give you the required length of bias binding for the bottom edge.

Measure the diameter of the table. Add ¾in to this measurement for seam allowances. This is the diameter of the top piece and equals the length of fabric required. If table is wider than fabric, you will need two lengths plus one extra pattern repeat for matching.

Making the tablecloth
□Cut out the circular piece for the tablecloth as for the short cloth. (Unless your table is wider than 48in you will not need to join lengths of fabric.) Cut the length of the ruffle, then cut along one side of the fabric to get the correct depth.

Measure the distance from the table top to the floor and add ⅜in for the seam allowance. This is the total depth of the ruffle and it should be cut from the width of the fabric.

Making bias binding

☐ Bias binding is used to neaten raw edges and to produce a decorative finish. It can be made from the same fabric as the main article, or in a matching or contrasting plain fabric. The advantage of bias binding is that it can stretch and go around curves without puckering.

☐ To find the bias grain, fold the fabric so that one selvage is at a right angle to the other selvage (from A to B) (fig. a).

☐ Cut along the fold line and cut 1in wide strips parallel to the first cutting line. One inch is wide enough for most purposes, but piping, for example, may require slightly wider strips (fig. b).

☐ Place the strips with right sides together and raw edges matching. Pin, baste and machine stitch ⅜in from the edge. Unfold the strip, press the seam open and trim the corners (fig. c).

☐ Turn under ¼in to the wrong side of the fabric along each edge and press well (fig. d).

☐ Unfold one edge of the binding and place it along the raw edge of the fabric, right sides together and raw edges even. Pin in position. Baste and machine stitch along the foldline (fig. e).

☐ Fold the binding over to the wrong side of the fabric. Slipstitch by hand along the original seamline, or machine stitch ⅛in from the edge (fig. f).

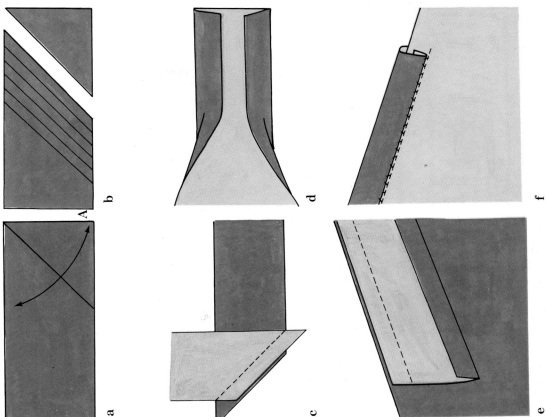

B

A

a

b

c

d

e

f

Making the ruffle

☐ With right sides together, pin, baste and machine stitch the short sides of the ruffle, taking a ⅝in wide seam allowance. Finish the raw edges and press the seam open.

Using the longest stitch length on your sewing machine, make a double row of stitching ⅜in from the top edge of the ruffle. Carefully pull up the bobbin threads of the two gathering rows until the ruffle is the right size (fig. 6).

At the ends of the gathering, wind the threads around a pin in a figure eight to facilitate the final adjustment of the gathers.

☐ With right sides together and raw edges even, pin the ruffle to the top piece, making sure that the gathers are evenly spaced. Baste carefully and machine stitch ⅜in from the edge. Remove the basting thread and press the seam allowances toward the top piece; trim and finish raw edges. Finish the edge of the ruffle with bias binding as for the short cloth (fig. 7).

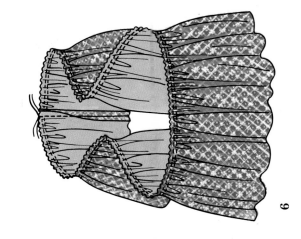

6

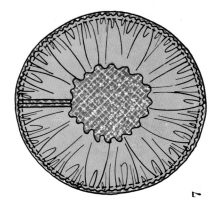

7

Embroidered Tablecloth

Embroider this beautiful tablecloth and bring the charm of traditional needlework into your home.

Finished size
60in square

Materials
1¾yd of 72in-wide linen
Five skeins of stranded embroidery floss in pale green
Four skeins of stranded cotton embroidery floss in pale yellow
Small pearl-colored red luster washable beads
Matching sewing thread
8in-diameter embroidery hoop

Tracing paper
Dressmaker's carbon paper

□ From linen cut out a 60in square.

□ Trace the motif from the trace pattern shown below. Using dressmaker's carbon paper mark the motif on the right side of the fabric. Place a motif in each corner of the fabric square, 7in from the corner point and 4¾in from side edges (fig. 1).

□ Place the motif area of the fabric that is to be embroidered within the embroidery hoop and pull the fabric quite taut. Use three strands of embroidery floss throughout: green for leaves and stems and for stitching on beads, and yellow for flowers (fig. 2).

□ Sew the flowers in fishbone stitch, completing one petal at a time. Bring the floss through the fabric at A and make a small straight stitch along the center line of the petal. Bring the floss through again at B and make a sloping stitch across the central line at the base of the first stitch. Bring the floss through at C and make a similar sloping stitch to overlap the previous stitch. Continue, stitching each side alternately, until the petal is filled (fig. 3).

□ In the center of each flower, stitch three beads (fig. 4).

□ Sew the stems in chain stitch, intertwining the lines of stitching. Bring the floss out at top of the line and hold down with your left thumb. Insert the needle into the fabric where it last emerged and bring the needle point out a short distance away along the line of the design. Pull the thread through, keeping the working thread looped under the needle point (fig. 5).

□ Sew the leaves in fishbone stitch, in the same way as the flower petals, but make the shape of each leaf more pointed, by slanting the stitches at a sharper angle. Stitch each leaf so the base is attached to the stem (fig. 6).

□ Stitch three beads in neat clusters around the motif (fig. 7).

□ Sew each motif in the same way in each of the four corners of the tablecloth. Embroider single flowers at intervals between each corner motif along the sides of the tablecloth, 4¾in from the edge. Sew them in the same way as in the large flower motif, adding beads in the center.

□ To finish the outer edges of the tablecloth, machine stitch a scalloped edge, using pale green sewing thread. Trim away excess fabric. Or finish by turning a double narrow hem all around the

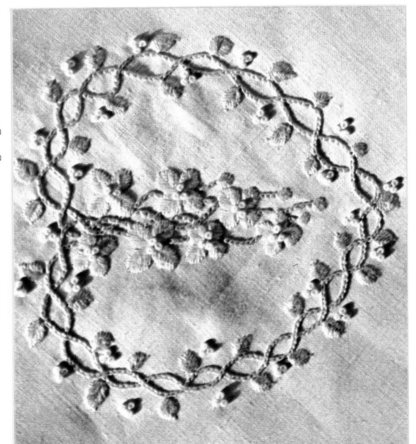

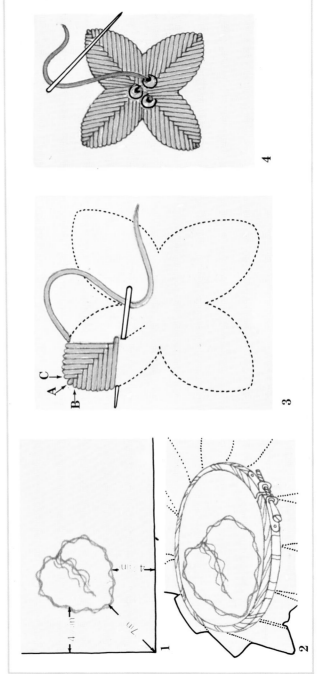

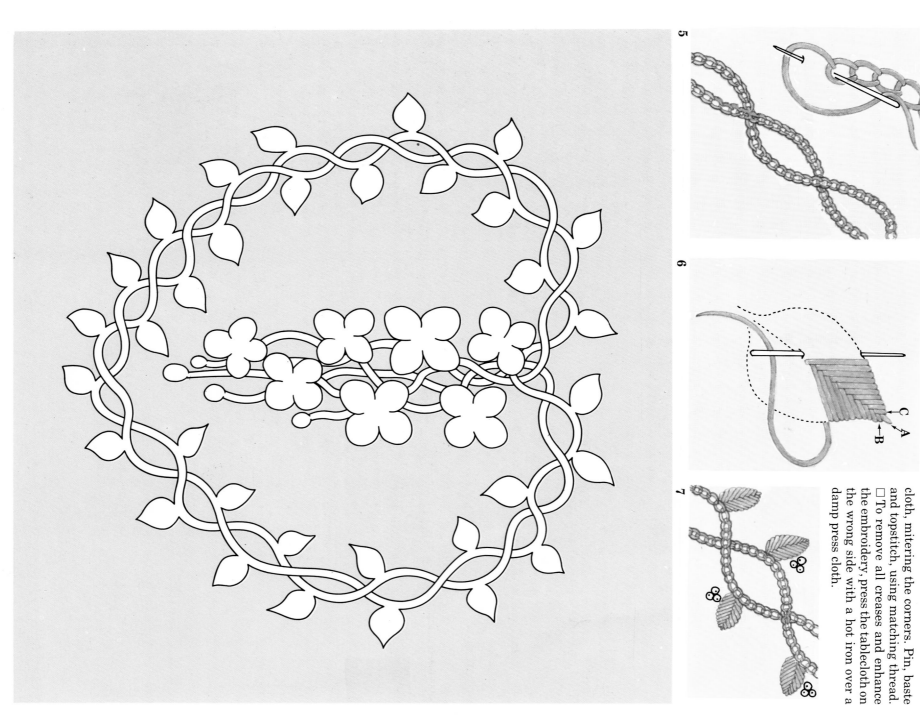

5

6

7

cloth, mitering the corners. Pin, baste
and topstitch, using matching thread.

☐ To remove all creases and enhance
the embroidery, press the tablecloth on
the wrong side with a hot iron over a
damp press cloth.

Cherry Blossom Tablecloth

Even the simplest meal will become more festive when you use this charming cloth, made with basic stitches.

Finished size
As purchased tablecloth
Materials
Plain white cotton or fine linen table-cloth, approximately 4ft square; you could use a round, oblong or oval cloth cloth
6 skeins stranded embroidery floss in salmon pink; 1 skein each in pale blue; yellow-orange; brown; and sage green
Crewel needle, size 6
Tracing paper
Dressmaker's carbon paper
Wooden embroidery hoop

□ Trace the cherry blossom design on a sheet of tracing paper. Transfer the design onto each corner of the table-cloth, using a piece of dressmaker's carbon paper slightly smaller than the tracing paper. Lay the carbon paper on the cloth at one corner and lay the tracing on top of it, checking that the motif is positioned centrally across the corner. Pin the corners of the tracing paper to the cloth (fig. 1). Trace over the design with a pencil. Repeat for the other three corners.

□ On another sheet of tracing paper, draw a circle about 18in in diameter and mark the center. Divide the circle into six equal segments and mark dots around the perimeter. Center the line and arc of the circle for each segment over the blossom design and trace it. You should end up with a wreath of blossoms evenly spaced around your circle (fig. 2)

□ Find the center of the cloth by folding it crosswise and then lengthwise and marking the point where the folds intersect with a pin. Matching the center of the circle to the center of the cloth, transfer the design to the cloth as you did the corner motifs.

□ Make sure your embroidery hoop is clean, so that it will not leave a mark on the fabric. Place one corner of the cloth over the inside ring and push the outer ring over it. Adjust the screw on the ring to make sure the fabric is taut (fig. 3). Following the stitch and color guide, complete all embroidery within the area of the hoop.

□ First embroider the petals, using three strands of floss in salmon color. Bring the needle up to the right side at the edge of one petal. Sew satin stitch closely across the shape, making sure the transfer line is covered and the

edges neat. Fill in all the petals within the hoop in the same way. Note that the direction of the stitches varies from petal to petal on each flower (fig. 4).

□ Using three strands of brown floss outline the stems within the hoop area in stem stitch. Work from left to right on the design with small overlapping stitches (fig. 5). Using stem stitch, outline the leaves in green.

□ Using three strands of blue, embroider French knots where shown on the design. To make a French knot,

bring thread through from the back of the cloth at the required position. Holding thread down with your left thumb, wind needle around it twice (fig. 6a). Still holding thread tight, twist needle around to starting point and re-insert it close to the point where the thread emerged. Pull thread through to back and secure to complete a knot or re-insert it at the point where a nearby knot is to be made (fig. 6b).

□ Using three strands of yellow-orange stitch the remaining French knots.

Move the hoop to another corner of the cloth and work the same design there.

□ After finishing corners, move hoop to center and embroider wreath design, moving hoop around circle as you complete each section.

□ When all the embroidery is completed, press the tablecloth on the wrong side with a steam iron or use a dry iron with a damp cloth, first placing it over a folded terry cloth towel. The layer underneath will help to make the stitches stand out against the cloth.

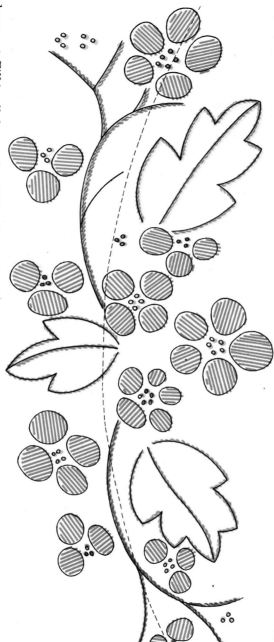

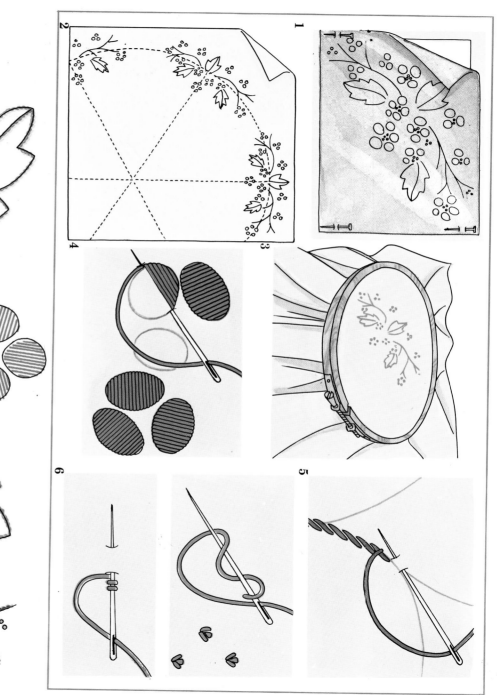

Cutwork Tablecloth

This beautiful cloth is embroidered using a swing-needle sewing machine. Pick solid color cotton fabric and a slightly darker sewing thread for an elegant result.

Finished size
60in-diameter circle

Materials
1¾yd of 90in-wide solid color cotton sheeting fabric
14 spools of slightly darker sewing thread
Embroidery hoop
Tracing paper
Dressmaker's carbon paper
30in-square sheet of white paper
Sharp-pointed scissors

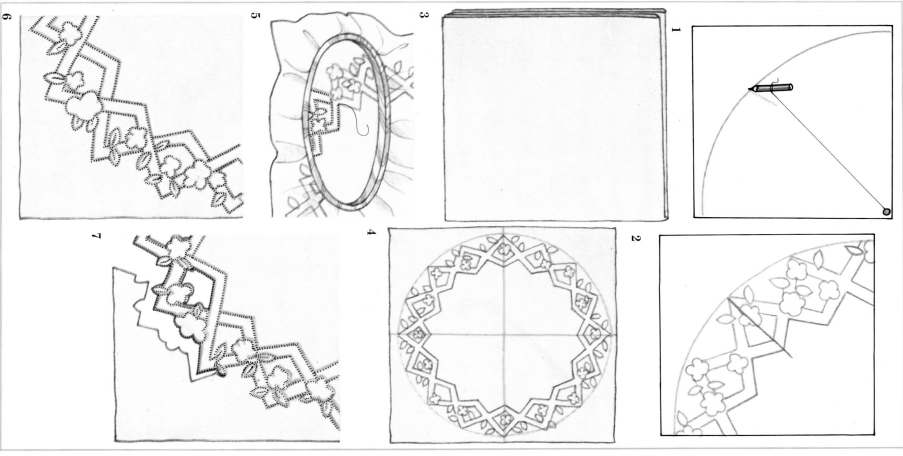

☐Trace the design shown on pages 137—39, matching green broken lines to :omplete one section of the design.

☐On the sheet of white paper draw a ,uarter circle, using string and a pencil. Fasten one end of the string around a thumb tack. Tie the string around the pencil, with the string 29½in long. Fasten the thumb tack in one corner of the paper. Keeping the string taut, draw an arc from corner to corner. This forms one quarter of the tablecloth pattern (fig. 1).

☐Mark the traced design section twice onto the white paper pattern: mark the section once, then remove the tracing paper and mark again to complete the quarter, realigning the design with the edge of the first section. This forms the pattern for one quarter of the table-cloth (fig. 2).

☐Cut the fabric to make a piece 60in square. Fold the fabric in half and then in half again and finger-crease the fold-lines to give quarters and also to mark the center point of the tablecloth (fig. 3).

☐Open out the fabric and place it on a firm surface. Place the dressmaker's carbon paper and then the white paper pattern over one quarter of the fabric. Match the corner point and straight sides of pattern to center point and foldlines of fabric. Mark the pattern. Repeat at each quarter to give the complete tablecloth design, adjusting if necessary to fit (fig. 4).

☐Embroider each part of the design with the help of an embroidery hoop. Stretch a section of the fabric to be embroidered in the wooden hoop, so that it lies flat on a working surface (fig. 5).

☐Set your sewing maching to ⅛in zig-zag stitch with the minimum length so that a solid line of satin stitching is worked. Remove the presser foot temporarily and place the embroidery hoop with the area to be stitched on the bed of the machine. Replace the presser foot and lower it to begin stitching. Carefully sew lines of satin stitch over all the lines of the design. Sew the lattice work first then the leaves, stems and flowers within the area of the hoop. When repositioning the hoop to the next part of the fabric to be embroidered, remember to remove the presser foot to take the hoop away from under the maching sewing area. Finish off all the loose threads each time you reposition the hoop. Continue around the

Note The actual-size pattern shown here and overleaf go together to make one-eighth of the tablecloth design. Draw the pattern onto tracing paper, matching the green lines together to complete the section.

tablecloth until all the design has been embroidered (fig. 6).

☐ Press the embroidery carefully on the wrong side of the fabric.

☐ Using a pair of sharp-pointed scissors, carefully cut away the excess fabric from around the tablecloth and also from within the diamond shapes of the lattice work (fig. 7).

☐ Press and starch the wrong side of the tablecloth to make the embroidery more pronounced and to give a firmness to the cutwork flowers and leaves so they will hang well.

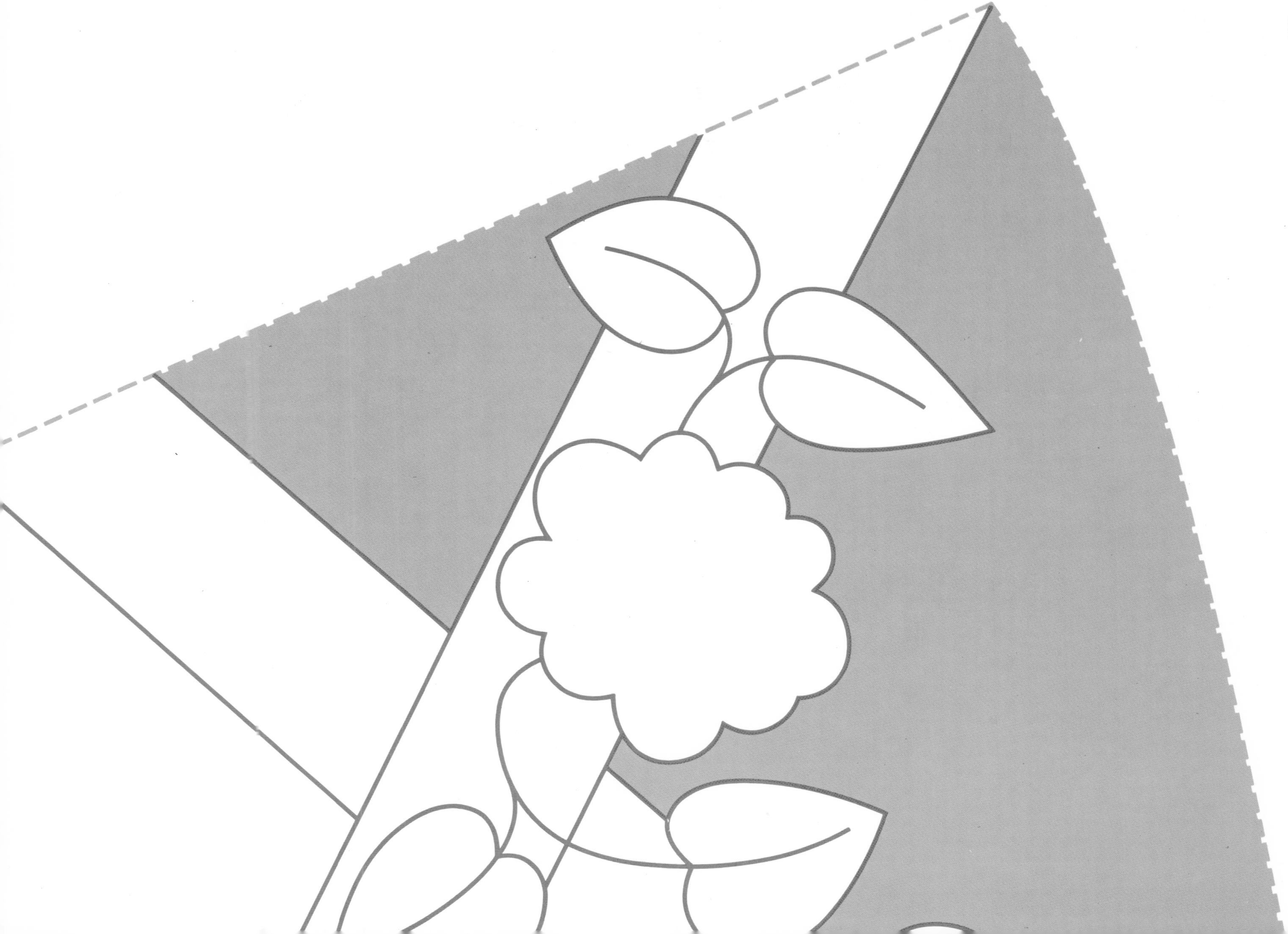

Patchwork Place Mats and Napkins

Clamshell patchwork is based on curves and can be an especially challenging motif to work – and especially stunning in its results!

Finished size
Each place mat measures 15½in by 11in

Materials
Eight 16in-square solid color linen napkins
¾yd of 36in-wide solid color cotton fabric for backing
⅝yd of 36in-wide cotton fabric in three different prints
Thick cardboard for patterns
Tracing paper
Sharp mat knife
Firm paper
5½yd of piping cord
5½yd of ½in-wide bias binding in contrasting color to napkins
Matching sewing thread

Note There is a trace pattern on page 143. If you prefer, buy a 3in pattern and a matching window pattern.

Preparing the patches

☐ Trace the two patterns: a window pattern for cutting out fabric patches (following the broken line) and a plain one for cutting out paper patterns (following the solid line).

☐ Mark the smaller, plain pattern only on thick cardboard and cut it out accurately using a sharp knife.

☐ Mark both pattern outlines, the smaller plain pattern inside the larger window outline, on the cardboard. Cut out around the outer line accurately, using a sharp knife. Also, cut around the inner marked line and discard the center piece, to provide a window.

☐ Place the smaller pattern on the firm paper. Draw around it accurately. Cut out the patch carefully (fig. 1). Repeat to make about ninety paper patches.

☐ Using the window pattern, draw around and cut out a selection of patches from the three different print fabrics; position the pattern on the wrong side of each fabric, lining the base of the patch with the straight grain of the fabric. This will make it easier to cover the paper patterns with the fabric. The window enables you to judge which part of the design will show (fig. 2).

☐ Pin a paper pattern centrally to the wrong side of a fabric patch. Turn the fabric edges over the paper pattern and baste down all edges. It will be necessary to clip the side curves to produce an accurate shape (fig. 3). Cover all the paper patches in the same way.

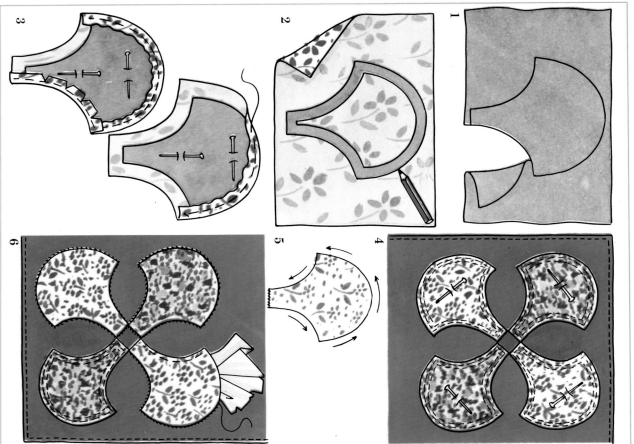

Napkins

□Use four clamshell patches for each napkin. Choose the patches to be used and arrange four in the corner of one napkin. The stalks of the four clamshell patches should just touch one another in the center of the motif. Pin and baste each patch to the napkin (fig. 4).

□With thread that matches the napkin, sew small slipstitches around each patch. It is advisable to stitch the base lines of the stalks first to ensure a neat square in the center and then to stitch the side curves (fig. 5). Before stitching each patch along the top curve, remove the basting stitches and carefully ease out the paper patch (fig. 6). Continue to stitch, tucking in the overlap to keep the curved shape. When the stitching is complete, press napkin on wrong side.

□Repeat to make three more napkins in the same way.

Place mats

□Press one remaining napkin flat.

□To draw the pattern for the place-mat, cut out a piece of tracing paper 8in by 6in; fold it in half each way, creasing paper well, unfold paper and place one quarter over pattern on opposite page, matching creased lines with center-lines. Mark outer curved line and the guideline for the edge of the patch-work, then fold paper into quarters again. Keeping papers together cut around marked outer line. Unfold pattern.

□Place pattern on napkin, leaving a border at least ¾in wide all around for seams. Pin pattern in place. Baste around edge to mark seamline on napkin.

□Select the patches and arrange colors to your taste making a triangular pattern of five rows (fig. 7).

□Follow this arrangement and using white sewing thread, hand stitch the patches together, working from the wrong side. Hold the patches flat in the hand and, with each stitch, catch a small amount of fabric (but not the paper patches) from each patch along their common sides (fig. 8).

□Build up the section of patchwork until you have the desired shape. Press the work flat on the right side.

□Work another patchwork section in the same way to match, for the other end of the place mat.

□Using the tracing paper pattern as a guide for positioning the patchwork, lay each patchwork section over basted shape of place mat (fig. 9). Pin and baste around it.

□Slipstitch around top scalloped edges using thread to match napkin. Remove all basting and paper patches.

□Make sure all seam allowances are flat and that the patchwork lies smoothly on the mat. Press the mat on the wrong side. Baste around the marked seamline of place mat, securing free edge of patchwork sections.

□To make the piping, press the bias binding strip open, fold it around the piping cord with wrong sides together, and stitch along binding close to cord.

□Pin covered piping cord around the place mat on the marked seamline with place mat patchwork side uppermost, leaving a 4in opening in one long side, leaving a ⅝in overlap (fig. 10).

□To finish binding, unpick the stitch-ing of the overlapping end and back for ⅝in. Cut the piping cord, not the bias strip, to meet the other end of the cord exactly. Fold in ¼in of raw end on unpicked bias strip and wrap over the other end of piping to give a neat join. Slipstitch around the join in the bind-ing to neaten (fig. 11).

□Stitch binding in place along seam-line. Trim place mat, leaving ⅝in seam allowance.

□Using tracing paper pattern, cut out one mat piece from cotton backing fabric, adding ⅝in seam allowance.

□With right sides together, pin and baste the backing fabric to the patch-work side (fig. 12). Working with the patchwork side uppermost, stitch along the previous line of stitching, leaving a 4in opening in one long side.

□Trim away excess fabric, leaving ⅜in allowance, and clip curves care-fully. Turn place mat right side out. Turn in opening edges and slipstitch together. Repeat for other place mats.

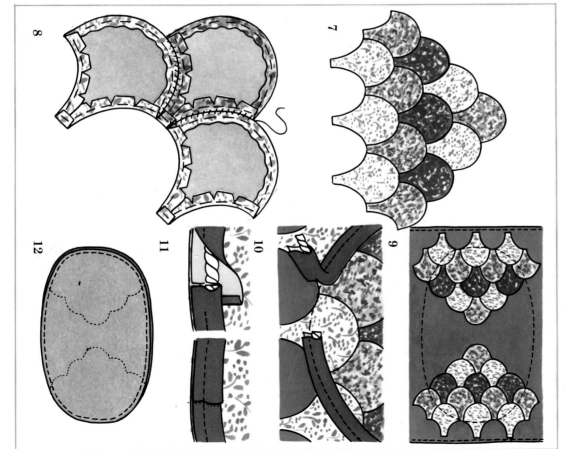

7

8

9

10

11

12

Quarter pattern of placemat.

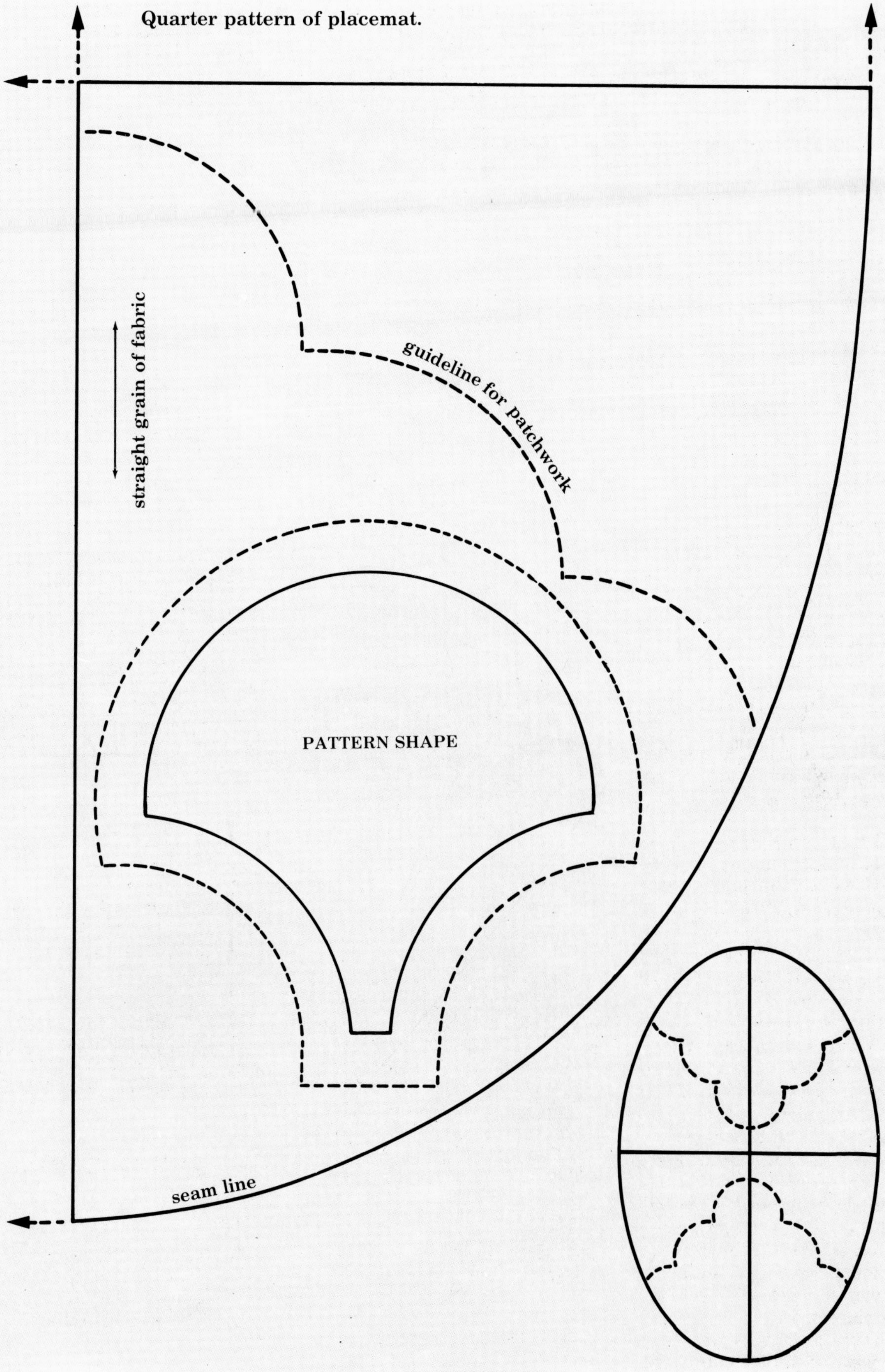

guideline for patchwork

PATTERN SHAPE

straight grain of fabric

seam line

143

Quilted Place Mats and Napkins

Give a stylish new look to your dining table with these attractive reversible place mats and coordinating napkins.

Finished size

Place mats 9 × 14in
Coasters 4in square
Napkins 17in square

Materials

For four place mats and coasters
½yd of 36- or 48in-wide floral fabric
½yd of 36- or 48in-wide check fabric
½yd of 36in-wide batting
7yd of ½in-wide bias binding
Matching sewing thread

For four napkins
1yd of 48in-wide fabric
Matching sewing thread

Choosing the fabric

☐ The most suitable fabrics are fairly firm cottons with sufficient body to make the napkins reasonably crisp. Firmness is also important for the mats, as the fabric will be less likely to stretch or become distorted when being quilted. Ensure that your fabrics, batting and binding are all washable. Choose a darker square check for practical everyday use on one side and a pretty toning print on the reverse for a special occasion.

☐ The mats are made with a layer of batting inserted between the two sides of fabric, which are quilted together by machine stitching along the lines of the check fabric. To complete the set, add napkins to match either side of the mats.

The quilting may be stitched in a contrasting color. This will make an attractive feature, but it will also highlight any unevenness in the stitching. It is often easier to achieve a profes-

sional finish by using a thread to match the background color of the fabric so that if there is a little unevenness in the stitching it will not be so noticeable in the finished item.

When cutting out the mats, make sure that the straight edges of the mats are parallel to the selvages of the fabric so that the quilting lines can follow the grain of fabric.

Making the place mats and coasters

☐ Following the fabric cutting layout (fig. 1), cut out four mats 9 × 14in and four coasters 4in square from each fabric. Cut each piece once from batting as shown in the batting cutting layout (fig. 2). Press the fabric pieces.

If you are not using a check fabric, mark out the quilting lines 1½in apart and parallel to the edges; mark with basting lines or very lightly with tailor's chalk on one set of fabric pieces.

☐ With the right sides outward, sandwich the batting between the two contrasting fabric pieces. Pin and baste around the edges and across the width of the mats at about 3in intervals along the quilting lines (fig. 3).

☐ Quilt the three layers together using a medium-length machine stitch. Following the lines of the fabric check (or quilting lines), stitch all the shorter lines first, working from the center line out to each side. Always start stitching at the same edge of fabric (fig. 4).

☐ Remove middle rows of basting. Complete quilting by stitching the second set of lines at a right angle to the first. Again start each row at the same edge (fig. 5).

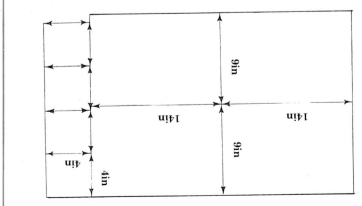

Place mats and coasters
Cutting layout for batting

Selvage

9in 9in 9in 9in

14in

Cutting layout for fabric

Selvage

4in

9in

14in

14in

9in

4in

4in

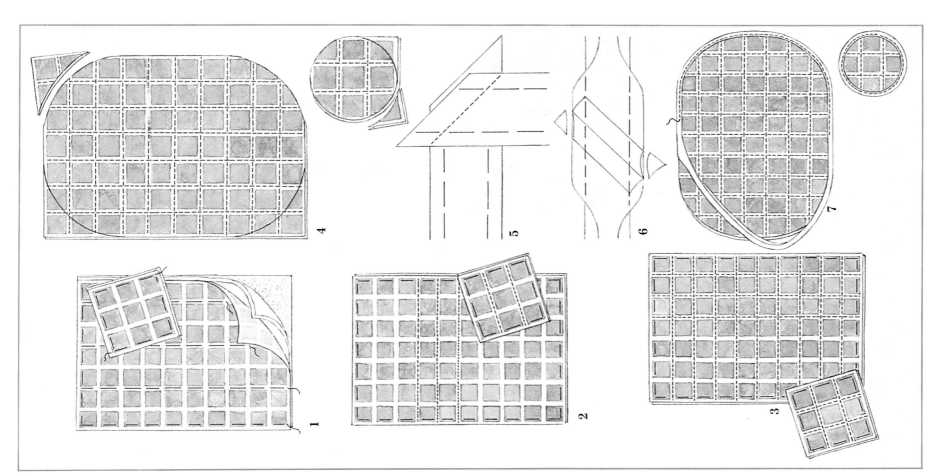

4

5

6

7

1

2

3

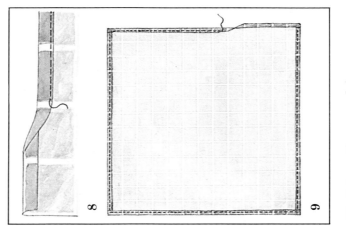

8

9

☐ Using a saucer, round off the corners of the mats. Trim corners and edges evenly. Using a small bowl, redraw coasters to a circular shape and trim (fig. 6).

☐ Cut bias binding to fit the edges of the table mats and coasters, allowing for ends to be joined along the straight grain. Unfold the binding at the ends and join together in the same way as bias strips are joined, make sure binding is not twisted before joining. Press seams open, fold and re-press binding as it was before. Fold binding in half lengthwise with upper folded half a little narrower than the under half (fig. 7).

☐ With the narrower half uppermost, insert the edge of the mat into the binding. Pin and baste in place through all thicknesses. Topstitch binding in place, and press binding only (fig. 8). If you have difficulty inserting the quilted edge of the mats into the binding, machine stitch around the edge of mats after trimming them to shape and before inserting edge into binding.

Making the napkins

☐ Cut out four napkins approximately 18in square; ½in hems are allowed.

☐ Press ¼in, then another ¼in to the wrong side along to opposite edges of the napkins. Machine stitch in place (fig. 9).

☐ In the same way press and stitch narrow hems along the remaining two opposite edges of napkins.

Chapter 5

Rugs and mats

Braided rug
Wrapped rug
Anemone rug
Cross-stitch rug
Rya rug
Picnic Blanket

Braided Rug

Use up all your fabric scraps in this braided rug. It is hardwearing and perfect for cheering up cold floors.

Finished size
About 40 × 33½in

Materials
Scraps of tweed and wool fabric,
in all about 7¾yd of 54in-wide fabric
Waxed cotton thread
Tapestry needle

□ From all the fabrics cut out 3in wide strips. Cut each strip on the straight grain and make them as long as possible. Fold each strip so that the raw edges meet in the middle of the wrong side of the fabric (fig. 1). Bring the folded edges of the strip together to make a flat strip with all the raw edges enclosed (fig. 2). Press each strip with a hot iron under a damp cloth (fig. 3). As you complete the strips, wind them around pieces of cardboard to keep them firmly folded, ready for braiding.
□ The rug is worked in a three-strand braid. To begin the braid, unfold the raw edges of two strips; pin, baste and stitch the two strips together. Stitch with right sides together and with a diagonal seam. Trim off the corner. Press seam open (fig. 4). Refold the strip, with the raw edges of the bias seam enclosed.
□ Position the third folded strip inside the first two strips at the seams, forming a T shape. Pin, baste and stitch the third strip firmly in place (fig. 5)
□ To work the braiding with the strips held taut, secure the T end either to a door handle or to a hook. This leaves both hands free for the braiding (fig. 6)

□ Start braiding by bringing the left-hand strip over the center and then bringing the right-hand strip over that strip (fig. 7). Continue braiding in this way, making sure that the folded edges of each strip are always toward the center of the braid. Be sure to keep the tension even, neither too tight nor too loose.
□ As the braid is formed, wind it around a piece of cardboard to keep it from tangling (fig. 8).
□ As a strip ends, join on a new strip, with a diagonal seam. It is an advantage if the strips are uneven in length,

so that bulky seams do not all fall in the same place in the braid. Braid over a seam join, so that it is hidden in the finished work. Braid a 7¾yd length before beginning to sew the braids together in the oval shape.

□ Lacing is the easiest and the strongest method of connecting the braids. Use a tapestry needle and strong cotton thread. Wax the cotton thread to make it stronger and keep it from knotting together while working.

□ To form the center of the oval, measure 12in of braiding, then turn the strip back against itself (fig. 9). Lace the turned-back strip of braiding to the center strip. Cut a length of thread and draw it through a loop of the braid. Knot the end and the working thread together to hold and slide the knot behind the loop. Draw the working thread through the corresponding loop of the braid opposite. Continue, diagonally up the braids, working through the corresponding loops of the braid (fig. 10).

□ Lace the braids together around and around the oval, keeping the braid flat.

Do not lace them together too tightly or the rug will curl up.

□ Continue to braid strips and sew them together around the oval until the rug reaches the finished size. As the end is approaching, start to taper the width of the braids by trimming the strips narrower. This will make the braid gradually blend into the last round of the rug.

□ Weave the remaining ends of the braid into the last round (fig. 11). Slip-stitch the ends invisibly to secure them in place.

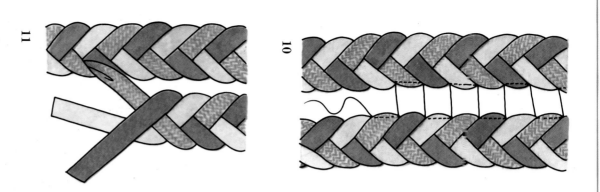

Wrapped Rug

Made in warm harmonious colors, this beautiful rug is simply cord covered with bands of rug yarn.

Finished size
About 37in in diameter

Materials
About 130yd of rug yarn in each of six harmonizing colors
(we used crimson, rose, scarlet, dark rose, deep cardinal red and plum)

Approx. 70yd of window sash cord
One reel of adhesive cloth tape
Two heavy-duty crewel needles
Adhesive

☐ Choose the starting color for the rug center and cut a 2yd length from the first ball of yarn.

☐ Take the first packet of sash cord and find the end. Wind one end of the length of yarn around and around the cord end tightly. Tuck in the raw end of the yarn and keep winding evenly around the cord, until you have covered a length about 3in long, which is long enough to be coiled (fig. 1).

☐ Thread the other end of the length of yarn onto one of the needles. Bend the bound end of the cord around into a coil.

Hold the coil tightly and draw the threaded needle through the center of the coil twice, pulling the yarn taut each time, to hold the coil in place (fig. 2).

☐ Lay the uncovered cord against the coil and wind the threaded yarn three times around the cord and then twice through the center of the coil. Repeat until you have worked once around the coil. This forms the center on which to work (fig. 3).

☐ Keep laying the uncovered cord against the previously worked section and wind the wool four times around the cord and then once into the previous row. This is the pattern, and is repeated continuously to make the rug (fig. 4).

☐ To change to a different color yarn or to add a new length to the same color, the same method is used. The changeover should take place when you still have about 8in of the working yarn left and at the beginning of the winding pattern. Cut a new length of yarn. Thread one end of the new length of yarn onto the second needle. Lay the unthreaded end of the new yarn length behind the cord and the working length, at the back of the rug. Work over the cord and the new length of yarn four times (fig. 5).

☐ Then take the new length and twist it around the old length at the back of

the cord. Then take the other end of the threaded needle through the center of yarn to produce the haphazard color scheme.

☐ Alternate bands of different colored yarn to produce the haphazard color scheme.

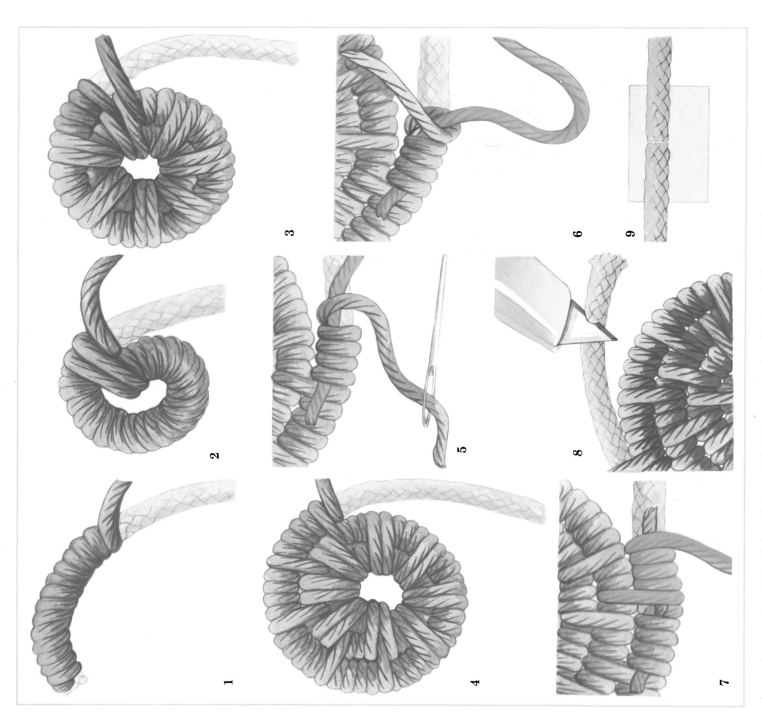

the cord, reversing their places. Take the new length of yarn and finish the pattern by working a stitch into the previous row in the normal way. Continue working in the same way with the new length of yarn.

□ Keep the old end of yarn at the back of the cord and work the next four rounds over it. Cut off the old length and continue as before with the new length of yarn (fig. 6).

□ To join on a new length of cord, trim off both ends of cord — the old and the new — with a sharp mat knife. Be careful to cut straight across the cord, not at an angle, so they butt neatly together (fig. 7).

□ Cut a 2in length of adhesive cloth tape. Place both ends of the cord centrally on the tape, so they meet in the middle. Put a dab of adhesive between the two ends (fig. 8). Roll the tape tightly around the cord ends once. Trim the tape and smooth in place.

□ When the rug is finished, trim away any excess cord. Place the end neatly against the last round and continue working over it until the cord end is covered. Weave the end of the yarn into the back of the rug.

□ Press the rug with a damp cloth and hot iron to smooth the rug completely flat. Brush if necessary.

Anemone Rug

This colorful design of brilliant anemones splashed across a yellow trellis makes a rug that emanates warmth – and gives you a luxurious and hardwearing addition to your home!

A hooked rug is a cosy and inviting addition to a home, and will last many years if finished properly. A strong binding stitched around the edge will ensure that the rug stays in shape and stands up to wear and tear. It will need to be durable if it is placed in a favorite, much used room. Lining with light-weight fabric, or latex rubber will add even more protection.

Stitched borders

It is possible to finish square and rectangular shaped rugs without adding a woven carpet binding.

□ Before hooking the rug, turn three rows of canvas around the outside edge to the right side, and overcast in place. Work through a double layer of canvas so the raw edge will be hidden by the pile. Selvages need to be trimmed away, as they prevent the hook from penetrating the canvas easily. Leave one row of unworked canvas around the outside edge.

□ When the hooking is finished, cover the exposed canvas with a binding stitch to create a border. Use a yarn of the same color and weight as the pile. Stitch into the row of holes adjacent to the pile, completely covering the vacant row of holes around the edge.

□ The overcast border and buttonhole stitch border are worked from the right side. Work the braided border with the back of the rug facing so the braided effect shows on the right side.

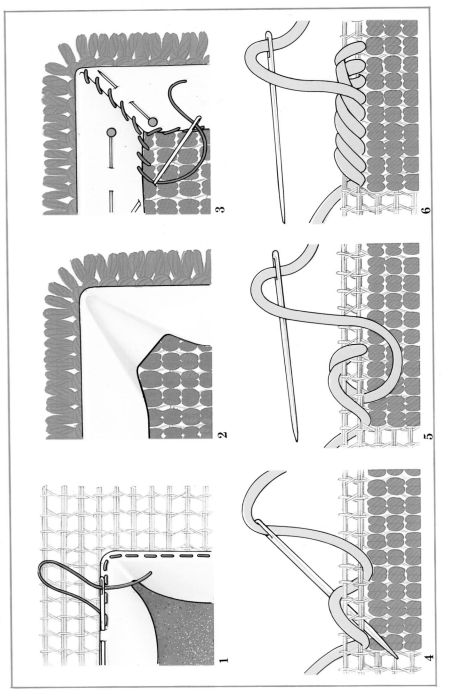

Binding the edges

□ For oval, circular and semi-circular rugs it is essential to use carpet tape to bind raw edges to the back of the canvas. Latex rubber is available in liquid form and should be applied before the carpet binding is stitched in place. The coated canvas is difficult to stitch through, so a sharp needle and heavy thimble should be used.

The width of carpet tape varies from 1 to 2in wide. It is available in neutral colors only, but can be dyed to match, if necessary.

A strip of unstitched canvas, approximately 1in wide should be left around the edge of the pile. The carpet tape is sewn to the excess canvas, then folded over and stitched to the back of the completed rug. Always allow for overlap and corner miters when calculating lengths of carpet tape.

Although it is not necessary, latex rubber can be applied to make the rug more durable and slip-proof. It also helps to anchor the pile firmly to the canvas.

Lining a rug

Hooked rugs can be lined with a sturdy tightly woven fabric, such as duck or twill. Button thread or heavy duty linen thread, and a sharp needle should be used for overcasting around the edges.

A lining can be stitched to a rug which has already been bound, or to one which has been hooked through the double layer of canvas finishing the edge, with or without a border. If the canvas has been finished without a binding after the pile is completed, it is best to add a lining for durability.

Stitch the lining to the rug on three sides only so that any dust and grit can be shaken out through the fourth and unattached side.

Sewing on a binding

□ Place the rug right side upward. Pin 2in-wide carpet tape to the edge of the unstitched canvas where it meets the pile. Sew the edge of the tape to the canvas, as close as possible to the edge of the pile (fig. 1).

□ Turn the rug over, right side down. Trim the corners of the canvas diagonally. Pull the tape and the unstitched canvas firmly over to the wrong side, making sure that no bare canvas is visible from the right side when the rug is finished (fig. 2).

□ Pin tape in place, keeping the canvas flat. Hemstitch the carpet tape securely to the wrong side of the rug.

Miter each corner. Take care not to allow pleats or corners to make unsightly bulges (fig. 3).

Braided border

□ Work with the wrong side of the rug facing. Bring the needle from back to front through the first hole on the left. Then, take the needle over to the back and through the fifth hole to the front (fig. 4).

□ Take the needle over to the back and bring it to the front through the next vacant hole on the left of the rug canvas (fig. 5).

□ Continue in this way, filling every hole in sequence until a thick border covers the canvas edge completely (fig. 6).

Buttonhole stitch border

□ Work with the canvas edge toward you, and from left to right. Place the needle through the hole to the back of the work, then down and over the working thread, forming a long straight stitch with a looped base line (fig. 7).

□ Continue in this way, working two or three stitches into each hole until the canvas is completely covered (fig. 7).

Overcast border

□ Bring the needle from the back through the first hole. Then take the needle back over the canvas and work the next stitch in the same way. Work three stitches into every hole to ensure canvas is covered (fig. 9).

Sewing on a lining

□ Trim the excess canvas around the pile to 1in. Fold to the wrong side of the rug and overcast to secure (fig. 10).

□ Cut out a lining 1in larger all around than the finished rug. Pin the lining to the back with wrong sides together. Place pins at various points over back of rug with edges left free (fig. 11).

□ Turn in and miter each corner of the lining. Pin the corners in place keeping the lining as smooth as possible without stretching it (fig. 12). Turn under the side hems and pin in place. Overcast three of the hems to the back of the rug (fig. 13).

□ Hem the lining of the fourth side without sewing it to the rug (fig. 14).

Buttonhole stitch border

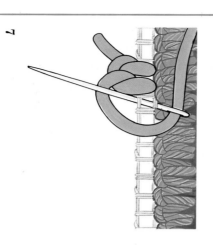

7

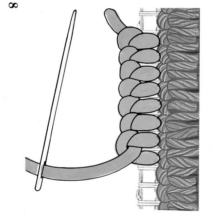

8

Overcast border

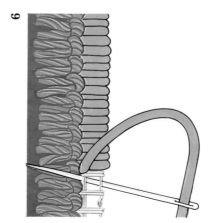

9

Making the anemone rug

Finished size

36 × 54in approximately

Materials

1¾yd of 48in-wide rug canvas
(10 holes to 3in)
A thick rug yarn in pre-cut packs
(based on packs of 240 pieces each):
52 of shade 16; 9 of shade 14; 7 of
shade 21; 6 of shade 17; 5 of shade 13;
4 of shade 22; 4 of shade 20;
4 of shade 25, 3 of shade 15
Latch hook
1¾yd of 48in-wide duck or
evenweave linen
5¼yd of 2in-wide carpet tape
Button thread
Sharp darning needle
Thimble
Rug scissors

□ Trim the canvas to 130 holes wide and 194 holes long. Fold over to the right side 5 rows of holes at each raw edge, and overcast to secure.

There should be 120 × 184 rows of holes to be worked, and each edge of the canvas should be hooked through a double layer.

Making the rug

□ Place the canvas in your lap and keep it flat. Simply follow the chart, making hooked knots one row at a time across the canvas from side to side. Begin from the bottom and work upward. It is possible to begin from the center or from either side, but still work upward. This will ensure that the tails of completed stitches fall down over those below them, giving a uniform pile.

□ Turn the canvas over from time to time and check that a knot is worked around each strand of canvas. It is very easy to miss out a strand because the canvas becomes obscured by the pile as you work.

□ When a few rows are complete, fold the canvas already stitched face down over your knees, leaving the next row which is to be hooked in front of your hands.

Finishing

□ When the design is completed, turn the rug over, wrong side facing. Sew on the binding tape as shown in the instructions.

□ Pin the lining fabric to the back of the rug, and trim as shown. Stitch the lining to the rug by overcasting, leaving one hem free. Add the finishing touch by carefully clipping the pile with rug scissors.

□ When the stitched border is complete, fasten off the yarn and then thread the ends along inside the border itself for approximately 4in before cutting off the ends.

□ This will prevent a lumpy knot which might unravel with wear and tear.

Working diagram for rug

Rug size 36 × 54in (120 × 184 holes)

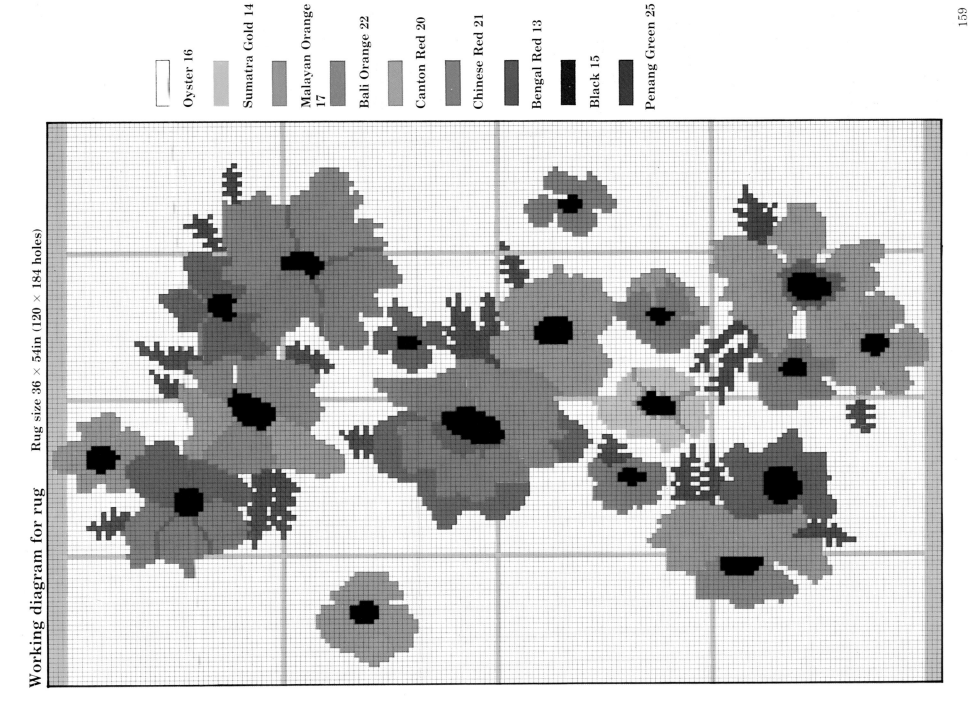

Oyster 16

Sumatra Gold 14

Malayan Orange 17

Bali Orange 22

Canton Red 20

Chinese Red 21

Bengal Red 13

Black 15

Penang Green 25

Cross-Stitch Rug

Work this vibrant rug in wool and it will be a long-lasting and much admired feature in your home.

Finished size
About 48 by 27in

Materials
1½yd of 27in-wide rug canvas with 6 holes to 1 in (larger gauge canvas can be used, but the rug will be larger)
Rug yarn in the following colors and quantities: 175yd in medium green; 90yd in orange; 65yd in each of emerald green, peacock blue, bright pink, pale blue and pink; and 45yd in bright yellow
One large tapestry needle

□The rug is worked in cross stitch with a cross worked over one canvas intersection. Make sure that the upper half of each cross you have made lies in the same direction (fig. 1).

□Turn under four rows of canvas along one short edge. Begin stitching the rug at this short edge, stitching the first four rows through both layers of the canvas (fig. 2).

□Work a few rows the same width in the same color along both the long edges to position the design on the canvas (fig. 3).

□Continue working the design of one quarter of the rug following the diagram which shows all the colors on pages 162–63.

□Work the same number of stitches along the left-hand edge to the center of the diagram, as the number worked on the short edge.

□Complete one half of the rug, by reversing the diagram, remembering that the double broken lines indicated on the diagram mark the center stitch (fig. 4).

□Complete the rug by working the second half, again reversing the diagram. Leave the last four rows of the design unworked.

□Turn under the surplus canvas four rows from the end to the wrong side of the rug. Work the last four rows through both layers of canvas in mid-green. Trim off any surplus canvas left over beyond the stitching.

□Work binding stitch in mid-green along both long edges of the rug (fig. 5). Work with wrong side facing. Work a few upright stitches, then insert needle in first hole (A) and bring it toward you; go over to fourth hole (B), back to second hole (C), then forward to fifth hole and so on.

□Work whip stitch in mid-green along both short edges of the rug, to cover the folded canvas edge (fig. 6).

□Press rug with damp cloth; pull into shape.

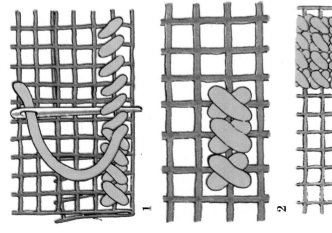

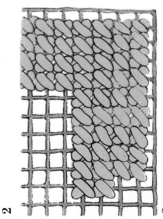

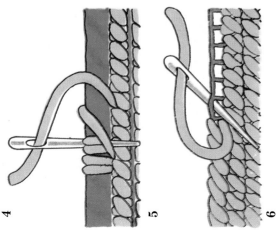

1

2

3

4

5

6

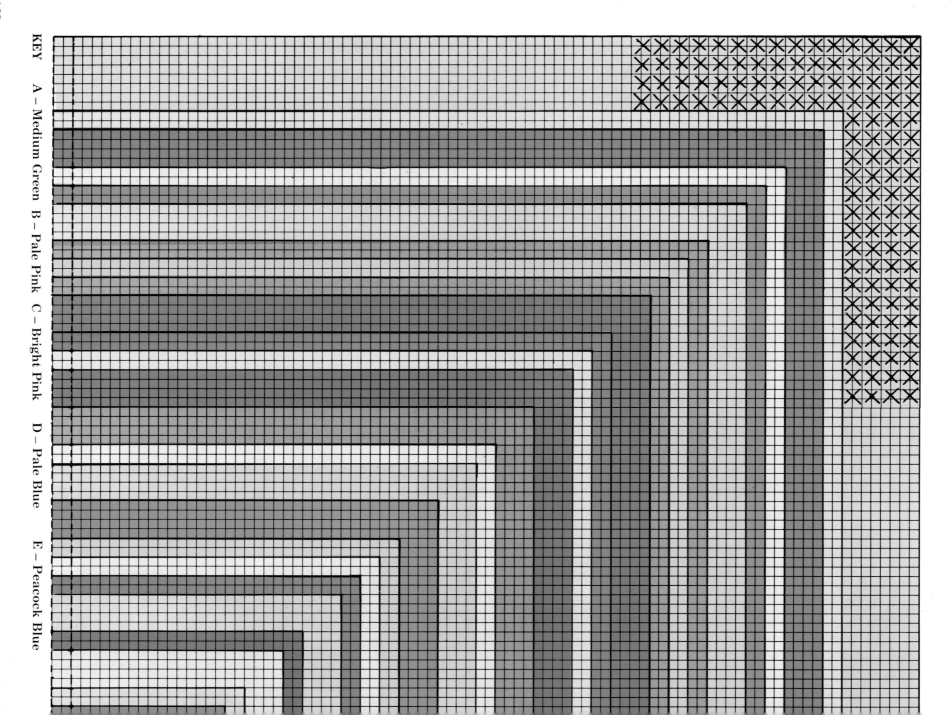

KEY   A – Medium Green   B – Pale Pink   C – Bright Pink   D – Pale Blue   E – Peacock Blue

F – Orange   G – Bright Yellow   H –.Emerald Green

163

Rya Rug

In the Middle Ages, rya – from *ryijy*, the Finnish for shaggy – described heavy cloaks made from fleece inserted into coarse cloth. Modern Finns use the same technique with yarn and canvas to make shaggy rugs, pillows and bedspreads. Choose blocks of color for a modern look.

Finished size
36 × 30in approximately

Materials
Rya rug wool:
20 packs (240 pieces each) in each of 5 colors, main shade (A), contrast colors (B), (C), (D) and (E)
Rya canvas, measuring approx. 38 × 32in
Latch hook

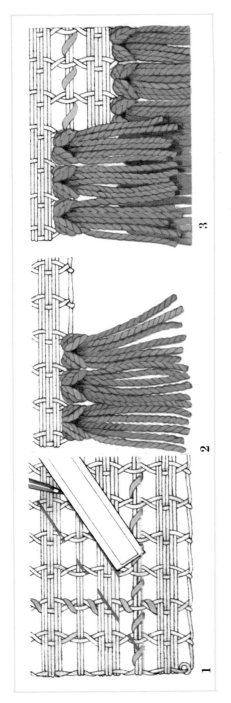

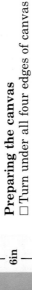

□ Although it is possible to use scraps of knitting yarn, rya rugs are best made from the special two-ply yarn made for this purpose. The yarn is usually sold in packs of 240 pre-cut. strands, each strand measuring about 7in in length and producing a knotted pile approximately 2¾in long. Because the pile is longer than that of normal latch-hook rugs, there is no need to work the knots so closely together. On rya canvas, therefore, the weft (crosswise) threads are woven in alternate groups of one and three, the knots being worked around the single threads. The vertical strands which separate the knots are twisted. Conventional rug canvas can be used if you knot along alternate horizontal threads.

Preparing the canvas

□ Turn under all four edges of canvas along single horizontal and twisted vertical threads so that the canvas measures 37½ × 30in. Baste the hems.

□ Using a waterproof felt-tip pen and following the diagram on this page measure and mark the design on the canvas.

Making the rug

□ Begin at the bottom left-hand corner and follow diagram for color sequence. Use the latch hook to knot three strands of yarn through all thicknesses of canvas around the single horizontal thread lying on the fold, so that the knots lie between vertical twisted threads.

□ *Miss the next group of three horizontal strands lying above the last row of knots. Work the next row of knots around the next single horizontal thread. Rep from * to the top edge, working the last row of knots around the single thread lying on the top fold. Turn the rug to the wrong side and work any knots omitted.

□ Since the knots are worked through all thicknesses of canvas on the edge of the rug, there is no need to bind the edges of the rug.

If you wish, you can back the finished rug with burlap; but if you decide to do this, you must not use the rug on a polished floor because it will slip very easily.

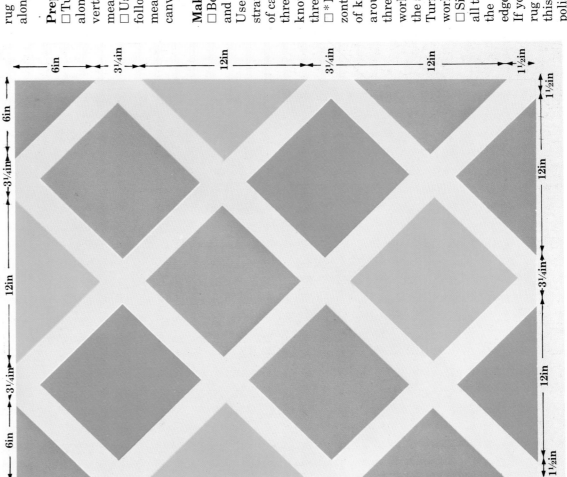

Picnic Blanket

Whether you take this blanket with you on picnics, or simply throw it over a bed or chair, it will come into its own and become a really useful household item.

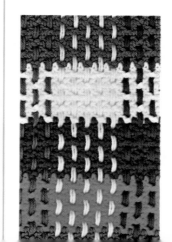

Finished size

69in long by 56in wide excluding fringe

Materials

Approximately 660yd bulky yarn in main shade, A

Approximately 580yd each of contrast colors B, C and D

J Size crochet hook

Large-eyed needle

Gauge

12st and 6 rows to 4in over patt on Size J hook.

Note To obtain an even background insert hook under 3 top strands of tr of previous row working into body of st.

Crochet pattern

Using J10 hook and A, make 174ch.

Base row Into 6th ch from hook work 1 dc. *1ch, miss 1ch, 1dc into next ch, rep from * to end. Turn. 85 spaces.

1st row 4ch to count as 1dc and 1ch, 1dc into next dc, *1ch, 1dc into next dc, rep from * to within last space, 1ch, miss 1ch, 1dc into next ch. Turn. The last row forms patt. Rep last row 3 times more. Cut off A. Cont in patt working striped sequence of 5 rows B, 5 rows C, 5 rows D and 5 rows A throughout until the 6th A stripe has been completed. Fasten off.

To complete

Sew in ends. Press lightly under a dry cloth with a cool iron.

☐ Cut 50 lengths of A and 40 lengths of each of B, C and D, all 88in long. Using 2 strands of A and beginning with first row of spaces, leave 6in of yarn free, then weave vertically over and under 1ch bars separating dc, taking care not to twist strands. Pass needle through first ch on lower edge, not into space and also through final ch at top edge to prevent yarn from slipping. Weave smoothly to leave 6in free at top edge (fig. 1).

☐ Work 4 more rows in A, weaving over alternate bars to preceding row. Following the striped sequence of rug, cont to weave over alternate bars until all bars have been worked over.

☐ Cut two 13in lengths of color required for each space along both edges of rug. Fold strands to form a loop. Insert hook into first space at lower edge, draw loop through, draw woven ends through loop then draw fringe ends through loop and draw up tightly.

☐ Rep along lower edge and upper edge, taking care to keep same side of rug on top while knotting fringe. Trim fringe.

Weaving

Thread a blunt-ended needle with two strands of yarn, cut to the required length. Insert needle through foundation chain: pull through leaving a 6in end. Working over and under chain bars insert needle through mesh from front to back and pull yarn through – so covering first chain bar: bring needle through mesh from back to front, then over next chain bar and through mesh from front to back. Continue in this way to top of mesh, insert needle through top of last row, remove needle and leave end free.

To work second row: insert needle through foundation chain, pull through leaving a 6in end. Take needle behind first chain bar and

bring through mesh from back to front, pull yarn through: take needle over next chain bar and insert through mesh from front to back, pull yarn through – so covering the chain bar. Continue in this way to top of mesh, insert needle through top of last row, remove needle and leave end free. These two steps are repeated to form rows of alternating weave.

Note *The needle is passed through the first chain on lower edge rather than into the space and also through the final chain in the top edge to prevent the yarn from slipping. Do not pull yarn too tightly, but weave at a tension that leave 6in free at the top edge.*

INDEX